AN INDEX TO
HISTORICAL FICTION
FOR CHILDREN AND
YOUNG PEOPLE

An Index to Historical Fiction for Children and Young People

≈

JANET FISHER

SCOLAR PRESS

Published by
SCOLAR PRESS
Gower House
Croft Road
Aldershot
Hants GU11 3HR
England

Ashgate Publishing Company
Old Post Road
Brookfield
Vermont 05036
USA

British Library Cataloguing-in-Publication Data

Index to Historical Fiction for Children
and Young People
    I. Fisher, Janet
    011.62

Library of Congress Cataloguing-in-Publication Data

Fisher, Janet.
    An index to historical fiction for children and young people /
compiled by Janet Fisher
        p.   cm.
    ISBN 1-85928-078-1 : $59.95 (approx.)
    1. Historical fiction, English—Bibliography.   2. Young adult
fiction, English—Bibliography.   3. Children's stories, English—
Bibliography.   I. Title.
Z2014.5.F57   1994
[PR830.H5]
016.823'081099287—dc20   94-896
                                                                     CIP
                                                                     AC
ISBN 1 85928 078 1

Typeset in 10 point Palatino by Manton Typesetters, 5–7 Eastfield Road, Louth, Lincolnshire and printed in Great Britain by Hartnolls Ltd, Bodmin.

To David, Lucy and Greg
with thanks for their love
and support

CONTENTS

LIST OF ILLUSTRATIONS

INTRODUCTION

All of us involved in working with children and books are aware that there is a large number of good historical novels for children, and that they remain unread by the vast majority of children and young people. The main reason that I compiled this index was to try to redress that balance, by providing a concise reference that improved the accessibility of those stories. Certainly as a school librarian I used it, often, and not just with history teachers and classes, but in work with English GCSE classes, exploring themes, in compiling project collections, and just as an answer to 'I'd like a good book, Miss'.

The main section lists over 460 books alphabetically arranged by author. It is followed by a title index and a detailed subject index. Some of these books are well known, and many more deserve to be better known. All have been published in the United Kingdom, although there is a number that were originally published elsewhere.

Each main entry gives full bibliographical details, including whether the book is out of print; where two sets of publishing details appear, the second refers to a paperback edition. Prices have not been included. The entry also includes a brief summary of the plot and an evaluation of the work, and also an indication of the age for which the book would be suitable (indicated in the entries as IR). Each book has been selected on its own merits, not because it is by a specific author or belongs to a particular series. Sadly, a large number of these books are out of print (o.p. in the entries), but good public libraries do have copies of them. I would like to think that some of those which certainly ought not to be out of print, are quickly brought back by publishers.

I have only included books dealing with history up to the end of the Second World War. Time-slip stories have not been included as these are a genre of their own, incorporating as they do an element of fantasy which does not belong in a true historical novel.

It is difficult to write an historical novel which makes the past come alive. Some writers can do it instinctively, Rosemary Sutcliff and Barbara Willard for example. There are so many pitfalls; the hero can be too modern in his thinking, or the dialogue can let a story down immediately. Ultimately the criteria for a good historical novel is the same as any other book, to create a world which the reader can inhabit for the length of the story. The difference with historical fiction is that the world is in the past.

To create that world is a matter of getting right the period details, costume, food, place, dialogue and the events that touch the characters' lives. The political and social background is especially hard to explain if the reader is not to be put off by too many indigestible facts. The best stories are those in which those facts emerge for the reader, much as they did for the characters who, it must be remembered, are usually children. A good example of this is *Johnny Tremain* by Esther Forbes, in which the reasons for the American War of Independence unravel along with the story of Johnny's involvement in it. Of course the events must be correctly portrayed and any bias noted. I have indicated where a one-sided view is given. Sometimes it is no bad thing, and gives the story a fervour perhaps not experienced in a perfectly fair account, but one must be aware of it and able to counterbalance it. Sometimes a fictitious plot, to kill Elizabeth I for example, is mixed in with real facts, which makes for a more exciting story, but this is a questionable method and can confuse the reader.

Place is more than usually important in historical novels, helping as it does to create a vivid past, and several writers have chosen to write of a particular area. Barbara Willard's Mantlemass novels, set in Ashdown Forest in Sussex, are eight linked stories in which the events in the outside world impinge slowly and some more than others. In *A Cold Wind Blowing* the dissolution of the monasteries affects Dick Plashet's life terribly, bringing him love and tragedy, but in *The Iron Lily* it is Lilias herself taking a man's place as Master of the Ironworks who makes mistakes in her own small world, unaffected by outside events. Above all, these are stories of a community brought together by its life in the forest and its dependence on it for their livelihood.

Sometimes it is through the domestic details of food and clothes that the past comes alive. Cynthia Harnett's stories, full of detail and with her entertaining drawings in the text, give a complete picture so that children can see themselves in the story. Laura Ingalls Wilder's books about her own childhood on the prairies dwell a great deal on food. I remember making cornbread after a spell of reading them because I had no idea what it tasted like and just had to know. The provision and preparation of food was an all-important task for survival, so it is right that these details should ring true. In *The Long Winter*, the account of the seven-month winter that the family spent in the small town on the prairies, the intense cold permeates the story and the reader can feel and see the snow on Laura's bed.

Period dialogue in particular is very difficult to convey without making the books too demanding to read. Rosemary Sutcliff achieves this with just the rearrangement of the words, which gives a slightly old-fashioned and stately feel to the prose that is exactly right for her stories of Roman Britain.

> 'A strange man you are, my lord,' Ness said. 'Three autumns ago you took me from my father's hearth as though I were a mere piece of household gear that you did not much want. And now you will let me go – you will let the child go – because I think you would fain have us stay.' (From *The Lantern Bearers*.)

It is so easy to get it wrong. I can well remember reviewing a book in which appeared the immortal words, 'Shut your mouth, you one-eyed troll'!

The characterization must be deep and true, and the reader must be able to care about and identify with the main characters. After all, if they are to provide the necessary link between past and present, the reader must be able to share in their problems, their happiness and sadness. But this of course is true for all stories. How, in *How's Business* by Alison Prince, evacuated to his aunt and uncle's in Lincolnshire, has to pass a test to be accepted by the local children at school. He worries about his Mum so travels to London to find her when he does not hear from her. Readers can feel they know How and share his problems.

Sometimes, however, it is very difficult to put yourself in a character's place; for example, the enormity of Misha's experiences in the Warsaw Ghetto is difficult to comprehend, but the reader can begin to understand how it must have been after reading *The Shadow of the Wall* by Christa Laird.

Illustrations can play an important part in a historical novel, helping to clarify details and events, and some of the very best artists have worked in this field. Maps are sadly missing from many books where they would have been very useful. It is amazing how many stories involving journeys or battles do not include what to me is a basic necessity.

It would seem that to bring the very distant past alive would be much more difficult because of the distance and lack of documentary evidence, but several writers have chosen this period, most notably Rosemary Sutcliff with her stories of Roman Britain and the early tribes who inhabited it. Henry Treece chose another early period, and with his sagas of the Vikings makes them real and credible people and destroys the barbarian label by describing them and their beliefs so vividly.

I feel very strongly that good historical fiction can illuminate the past for the young; that it can make that past seem nearer and more real, and therefore more relevant. Some of the very best writers for children and young people have chosen to write of the past, and it would be a tragedy if their work was to remain unread by future generations. I hope very much that this index will make the wealth of historical fiction for children and young people more accessible, and encourage them to read and enjoy it as much as I have.

Janet Fisher

LISTING BY AUTHOR

Gabriel ALINGTON

1 **Rumbelow Road**
Heinemann, 1979. o.p. 4349 2671 X

Mr Zakman is a figure of fun in Rumbelow Road in 1944, a
Polish Jew collecting old pieces of china, but when Matthew and Laura befriend him, they set up a shop to mend
all the broken bits. Mr. Zakman becomes accepted in this
way and when tragedy strikes it is seen as a way to begin
again. Matthew's father is dead and he and his mother are
working out their grief separately. A good picture of wartime London, the strong characterization making for a satisfying story.

IR 9+

Mabel Esther ALLAN

2 **An Island in a Green Sea**
Dent, 1972. o.p. 0 4600 5886 X

A story of an Hebridean childhood in the 1920s in which
Mairi sees her two brothers go to Canada, and her sister go
into service in Glasgow. The pain of all this is tempered by
the coming of Isobel, an English girl who wants to learn
Gaelic and stays to write a book about the Hebridean year.
The hardships of a crofter's life, the exodus of most of the

young people, the beauty of the landscape and the fierce weather are well described.

IR 10+

3   The Mills Down Below
Blackie/Abelard, 1980. o.p. 0 2007 2638 2

Elinor, the only daughter of a mill owner in the north of England just before the Great War, makes friends with a boy from the town, who paints a picture of a life unknown to her, in particular of school. Her cousin Amy, a suffragette, raises more questions, but Elinor's life changes with the onset of the war and the death of her father. This is an enjoyable read which does not explore issues to their fullest but which could well be used as a lead to more thought-provoking reading.

IR 10+

E. M. ALMEDINGEN

Almost all this author's books have a great love of Russia running through them, and give a strong picture of the life of the aristocracy and therefore a one-sided view of the time.

4   A Candle at Dusk
Illustrated by Doreen Roberts
Oxford, 1969. o.p.

A stark but moving story of a Frankish boy in eighth century Europe, who longs to be able to read. His father sends him to the Abbey at Ligugé to learn, but he is forced to return home when the Saracens advance, and he learns of the sacking of the Abbey, In the ruins he finds Dom Defenson's book which he can now copy and thus save. Dom Defenson is a real figure in a convincing story of life at its most raw, with hunger and ignorance being rife.

IR 10+

5 **Anna**
Illustrated by Robert Micklewright
Oxford, 1972. o.p. 0 1927 1337

In a romantic story based on the life of her great grandmother, the author tells of Anna's life as the daughter of an enlightened merchant living in a Moscow suburb at the end of the eighteenth century. Anna speaks six languages and learns to help in her father's business. Her brother is banished to England for marrying outside Russia, but Anna falls in love with a Russian and the story ends with her marriage. Details of Russian life abound and through the story runs the love of Mother Russia. Catherine the Great makes an appearance.

IR 10+

6 **Fanny**
Illustrated by Ian Ribbons
Oxford, 1970. o.p. 0 1927 1317 5

The story of the author's aunt taken largely from her own writings, tells of Fanny's childhood as the daughter of a Russian landowner through the years of the Crimean war, and after he loses his fortune, their move to France and later England. A loving portrayal of family life, with great wealth and the devotion of servants, but also of an enlightened master.

IR 10+

7 **One Little Tree: A Christmas Card of a Finnish Landscape**
Illustrated by Denise Brown
Parrish, 1963. o.p.

A charming story of a boy in a Finnish village close to the Russian border, after the Great War, who finds that because the border is closed he will not be able to acquire the usual tree from the Baroness' estate in Russia. Arni determines to get a tree and succeeds, finding kindness in a border guard. A good picture of Christmas customs of the time.

IR 7+

8   **Young Mark: The Story of a Venture**
Illustrated by Victor Ambrus
Oxford, 1967. o.p.

Set in the eighteenth century, this is the true story of a boy who journeys across Russia from his Ukrainian home because he feels he has a gift to sing; he wants to go to St Petersburg to see the Hetman, who is a Ukrainian (and who eventually becomes the morganatic husband of the Tsarina). The journey is vividly described and makes an exciting story, although a map would have been useful.

IR 10+

J.S. ANDREWS

9   **The Man from the Sea**
Bodley Head, 1970. o.p. 0 3700 1216 X

After all the men of his village disappear in a storm at sea, Evan finds a stranger on the shore. This man from far away saves the village of women and children from starvation by trading his bronze axe for food and then, with their help, mends his unusual boat and sets out with some of the children to find Evan's father. A moving, plausible story of early Bronze Age man with the central character a warm, compassionate man, a truly civilized being.

IR 10+

Elliott ARNOLD

10   **A Kind of Secret Weapon**
Longman, 1970. o.p. 0 5821 5009 4 (USA 1969)

A quite outstanding story of a Danish boy caught up in the work of printing an underground newspaper in occupied Denmark. The paper is printed by Peter's parents, and after his father is caught, tortured and killed, Peter and his mother take refuge and try to produce the last edition. A passionate plea for resistance to tyranny is made in this book with its portrayal of a close family upheld by moral principles.

IR 12+

Agnes ASHTON

11   **Water for London**
Illustrated by Monica Walker
Epworth, 1956. o.p.

An interesting and detailed account of the bringing of fresh water to London by goldsmith Hugh Myddleton, told through the medium of the adventures of Dickon who meets Myddleton by chance and comes to work for him. There is resistance and royal patronage, romance and adventure in a good solid story which occasionally catches fire. Useful for projects on water.

IR 10+

Gillian AVERY

12   **Call of the Valley**
Illustrated by Laszlo Acs
Collins, 1966. o.p.

A sad tale of a poor Welsh boy, living with his mother and drunken uncle, who leaves his valley to find a better life in Manchester. He returns home to find tragedy but also eventually, a brighter future. An interesting picture of a small Welsh community contrasting with the more prosperous society of Manchester in Victorian England.

IR 10+

13 The Elephant War
Drawings by John Verney
Collins, 1968. o.p.

Based on an actual event, the sale of an elephant to Barnum's Circus, this is a humorous look at what might have happened in Oxford in 1875. Harriet, impressionable only child of a doctor, gets caught up in a campaign to rescue Jumbo and meets the Smith boys, Thomas, Joshua and the incomparable James. Full of warmth and fun, and imparting an interesting picture of children's lives at that time.

IR 9+

14 Ellen and the Queen
With illustrations by Krystyna Turska
Hamilton, 1971. o.p. 2410 2089 1 (Antelope)

An entrancing story about Ellen Timms, always in trouble, who boasts that she will see the Queen (Victoria) when she comes to the big house, and how she makes her dream come true by seeing the Queen's legs! Lovely drawings by Krystyna Turska enhance this story.

IR 6+

15 Ellen's Birthday
With illustrations by Krystyna Turska
Hamilton, 1971. o.p. 0 2410 2090 5 (Antelope)

A spirited girl challenges the infringement of common rights to gather wood, largely to gather fuel to bake her birthday cake. Set in England in the 1850s. A slight story aimed at a young age group but which could well be used with older children.

IR 7+

16 **Freddie's Feet**
Illustrated by Krystyna Turska
Hamilton, 1976. o.p. 0 2418 9268 6 (Antelope)

Based on fact, this recreates how Freddie, dressed in skirts and curls, rebels by doing a headstand in front of Queen Victoria. A real gem of a story with sharp social comment evident in the difference between the family and the Blairs.

IR 7+

17 **The Greatest Gresham**
Illustrated by John Verney
Collins, 1962. o.p.

The three Gresham children, dominated by fear of their father's rages, meet up with Kate and Richard Holt and form a society to become great. In the end Henry becomes the greatest Gresham. The sympathetic portraits of the five children show clearly their place in Victorian society, their real physical discomfort from cold, and the truly Victorian attitude of their father. There are moments of great humour and pathos.

IR 9+

18 **James Without Thomas**
With drawings by John Verney
Collins, 1959. o.p.

An old-fashioned but warm and increasingly likeable tale of James and Joshua, who without elder brother Thomas, who is ill, stay with cousin Luke and meet with the Squerrye girls and the strange Lord Banbury. It imparts a fair amount of detail of the lives of nineteenth-century children, while still managing to be an amusing story of three boys together.

IR 9+

19   Jemima and the Welsh Rabbit
Illustrated by John Lawrence
Hamilton, 1972. o.p.

Jemima is a tomboy and when her father becomes a stationmaster in a sleepy Welsh village she thinks life will be dull. Then she meets Edward and with his help she decides they will make the Welsh Rabbit (a train) run on time. An attractive story, well told with humour, set in the 1870s.

IR 8+

20   A Likely Lad
Illustrated by Faith Jacques
Collins, 1971. o.p. 0 0018 4010 0

Willy Overs's father, a shopkeeper in Manchester at the turn of the nineteenth century, wants Willy to join the Northern Star Insurance company, but he wants to stay on at school. This difference between them leads to Willy running away, but an encounter with an earl and an old lady changes his father's mind. The scenes of family life and the awful Uncle Harold are beautifully drawn.

IR 9+

21   Mouldy's Orphan
Illustrated by Faith Jaques
Collins 1978. o.p. 0 0018 4512 8 (Young Fiction)
Puffin, 1981. 0 1403 1269 2

Mouldy reads a lot and from this gets the idea of giving a home to an orphan. She finds one on a trip to Oxford, but the plan backfires on her. Full of small details about life in Victorian England and of the warmth of Mouldy's family life in Canal Row, this slight tale (79 pages) would read aloud well.

IR 7+

22   **The Peacock House**
Illustrated by John Verney
Collins, 1963. o.p.

Kate's struggle to make a life for herself in a damp, uncomfortable house with her father, stepmother and stepbrother and sister makes a sad story, but, in spite of making some mistakes along the way, she wins through. Lady Guinevere and the ubiquitous Copplestone make an appearance in this story. As always with Gillian Avery the story is made by the interaction between the children but it also says a great deal about the place of children in Victorian society.

IR 9+

23   **Sixpence**
Illustrated by Anthony Maitland
Collins, 1979. o.p. 0 0018 4786 4 (Young Fiction)

Two boys play truant from school after earning sixpence working with the threshing machine. They sleep rough and get a lift with the baker's boy to a nearby town where they spend their sixpences, and pay for a ride back on the train to meet the wrath of their fathers. A wry, humorous look at life in a small Welsh community in the 1870s, pointing out in a short book the immense differences between these lives and those of a child nowadays, and including a look at the emergence of machines.

IR 8+

24   **To Tame a Sister**
Illustrated by John Verney
Collins, 1961. o.p.

Poor Margaret, harassed elder sister of Charles and Arthur, who dreams of being part of a literary gathering, finds it all comes to naught when they are sent off to stay with an eccentric aunt and uncle while their invalid mother is taken to Switzerland. Margaret is lonely and hungry while her brothers have a marvellous time and even find a source of

From R. Welch, *Sun of York*

food. Lovely exchanges between the three children and a humorous streak in the story make this a joy to read. Small details of the life of a Victorian child emerge.

IR 9+

25 **Trespassers at Charlcote**
With drawings by Dick Hart
Collins, 1958. o.p.

While staying in Oxford with their cousin Luke, the Smith boys meet the Squerrye girls. Joshua and Cordelia find a ruined house which they decide to try and rehabilitate. It is a rambling story, less successful than the others, but still full of the observations of the children's relations with each other and details of their lives in Victorian times.

IR 9+

26 **The Warden's Niece**
With drawings by Dick Hart
Collins, 1971. o.p.

The enchanting story of orphaned Maria, who runs away from school to her uncle in Oxford. He is the Warden of an Oxford college and she finds her way to his heart by her love of Classics. The Smith boys live next door and Maria joins them for lessons with the Reverend Copplestone. This humorous tale has much to say of the place of women and children in Victorian society.

IR 9+

27 **The Italian Spring**
Illustrated by John Verney
Collins, 1964. o.p.

The sequel to *The Warden's Niece*, slightly less successful in that it is rather sad, tells of Maria's visit to Italy after the Warden's death. She is ill in Venice and is only rescued from becoming a recluse by Cordelia (from *James without Thomas*), and then discovers the magic of Italy. A beautifully written story, subtly giving details of the position of women in Victorian England.

IR 9+

Margaret BALDERSON

28 When Jays Fly to Barbmo
Illustrated by Victor Ambrus
Oxford, 1968. o.p. 1 9271 2918

Ingeborg lives in German-occupied Norway on a remote farm with her father and her aunt. When her father is lost at sea, she discovers that her mother was a Lapp and meets her relations for the first time. The isolation of Ingeborg's life, particularly the dark winters, is beautifully described and her struggle and courage in coming to terms with her two worlds are well portrayed. A thoughtful book which requires some maturity from the reader, but well worth reading.

IR 12+

Martin BALLARD

29 Dockie
Longmans, 1972. o.p. 0 5821 5498 7

A stark tale of dockyard life in the England of the 1920s, telling of poverty and hardship and men trying to find work. Moggy thinks he has found a way out by becoming a boxer, but he is blacked by the union his father will not join and is forced to look elsewhere for work and, for a time, a home. The rough and raw life is reflected in the language used, but it is a riveting story.

IR 12+

R. BATEMAN

30 Jim's First Convoy
Illustrated by James Holland
Brockhampton, 1962. o.p.

Jim Marriott, an asthmatic boy who failed to get into his father's beloved Royal Navy, settles for the second best of the Merchant Navy. He trains as a radio officer and joins SS Waterloo on convoy duty. After being torpedoed the crew take to the boats, but return to the ship and eventually sink a submarine. It has echoes of a *Boys' Own* story, but would be useful with less able boys and is readable and exciting.

IR 10+

Nina BAWDEN

31 Carrle's War
Illustrated by Faith Jacques
Gollancz, 1973. 0 5750 1613 0
Puffin, 1974. 0 1403 0689 7

A marvellous story told with all Nina Bawden's skill. Carrie and Nick are evacuated to a Welsh village where Mr Evans and his sister take them in but he is an ogre and she is weak. The children find warmth and shelter at Druid's Bottom, the home of Mr Evans's other sister. Hepzibah, Johnny and Albert form a haven which all goes wrong when Mrs. Gotobed dies. Beautifully written, so that the reader is drawn into the world of a small Welsh village and the strange existence of an evacuee.

IR 9+

32 Keeping Henry
Illustrated by Joyce Powzyk
Gollancz, 1988. 0 5750 4256 7
Puffin, 1989. 0 1403 2805 X

Henry is a baby squirrel, found by Charlie and adopted by his mother, brother James, and sister (who narrates the story). They are living on a Welsh farm during the Second World War while their father is away in the Merchant Navy. Henry dominates their lives until he disappears towards the end of the story. The girl, who is away at school, finds returning to family life difficult and this is marvellously drawn.

IR 9+

33   **The Peppermint Pig**
Illustrated by Alexy Pendle
Gollancz, 1975. 0 5750 1927 1
Puffin, 1977. 0 1403 0944 6

Father loses his job through acting nobly and goes to America to seek his fortune, while Mother and the four children go to relatives in Norfolk and pass the time happily until he returns. They adopt the runt of a litter (the peppermint pig of the title) and Poll (the youngest) finds happiness and sadness. A warm story full of details of a late-Victorian childhood and a secure family life.

IR 9+

N. BENCHLEY

34   **Bright Candles: A Novel of the Danish Resistance**
Deutsch, 1975. o.p.

A story of how the Danes resisted the Nazi occupation as seen through the eyes of sixteen year old Jens, who started in a small way mimeographing newsletters and ended up a full blown saboteur. Death and tragedy are not glossed over and the courage of the Danes' resistance in large and small ways shines through.

IR 12+

Phyllis BENTLEY

35   The Adventures of Tom Leigh
Illustrated by William Stobbs
Macdonald, 1964. o.p.

In 1722 Tom Leigh, a weaver's son from Suffolk, travels north to find new work, but on the journey his father is killed. Tom, destitute, finds himself apprenticed to a clothier. Mr Firth who is bluff but kind. However, his journeyman weaver is a scoundrel and Tom finds out he is responsible for theft, and worse, for his father's murder. A spirited adventure story pointing out clearly the perils of being alone in the world at such a time.

IR 10+

36   Gold pieces
Illustrated by William Stobbs
Macdonald, 1968. 3560 2377 0

In Yorkshire in 1769, Dick Wade, a weaver's son finds a dog on the moor and meets Jaimie Hartley; both events which lead him into danger. Dick's home life and his learning of values ring true, and the picture of weavers and the coming of the flying shuttle are well drawn.

IR 10+

37   Ned Carver in Danger
Illustrated by William Stobbs
Macdonald, 1967. o.p.

A strong and powerful story of the Luddites, set in Yorkshire in 1812 against the background of the coming of machinery to revolutionize the making of cloth and in particular its finishing. There are fair portrayals of boss and worker, neither villains nor heroes, and the story is told in the first person by a boy who gets caught up in the movement.

IR 10+

38 **Sheep May Safely Graze**
Illustrated by William Stobbs
Gollancz, 1972. o.p. 0 5750 1356 7

After a stolid beginning imparting the complicated background of the Wars of the Roses, the story comes alive when Henry and Margery are on the run, and the details of shepherding on the Cumbrian fells are vividly drawn. Henry's restoration to his father's title and estates is movingly described.

IR 10+

Violet BIBBY

39 **Many Waters**
Faber, 1974. o.p. 0 5711 0549 1

Oliver Cromwell makes a brief appearance in this stark tale of resistance to change, and a grim life dominated by the landscape of the Fens. The Dutch come to drain the Fens, but are resisted. Constance falls in love with one of them and eventually they become handfast.

IR 10+

40 **The Mirrored Shield**
Illustrated by Graham Humphreys
Longmans, 1970. o.p. 5821 5022 1

Thomas, bastard son of a knight in the time of Henry VI, is brought up by his foster mother, a herbalist. Because he is left handed and therefore viewed with some suspicion by the locals he cannot be apprenticed in an old trade. However, the Master Mason sees his carving and takes him to help build the Old Palace at Croydon. There are glimpses of the larger world, of the Lollards, and much detail of ordinary life.

IR 10+

41 Tinner's Quest

Faber, 1977. o.p. 0 5711 1029 0

Jory, a tin miner's son in the Cornwall of the 1850s, goes to Australia to seek his father, who is deported to Van Diemen's Land and becomes involved in the gold rush there. The harshness of life at the time is not disguised, but the use of dialect makes for difficult reading. Would read aloud well.

IR 10+

42 The Wildling

Illustrated by Graham Humphreys
Longmans, 1971. o.p. 0 5821 5017 5

Set against the background of glass blowing in a seventeenth-century Wealden community, where Benet's gypsy blood from his mother makes him at home in the forest. One of the joys of this book is the description of the countryside, much enhanced by Graham Humphreys' lovely drawings. The decline of the glass blowing industry is clearly drawn.

IR 10+

Carol Ryrie BRINK

43 Caddie Woodlawn

Illustrated by Trina Schart Hyman
Macmillan, 1973. 0 0271 3670 (USA 1935, Newbery medal 1936)

A warm, loving account of a Wisconsin childhood in 1864 which follows Caddie through the year: full of details of everyday life, punctuated by excitements such as the Circuit Rider's arrival and the possibility of an Indian massacre. There is not much sense of the drudgery and hard work of frontier life, but a great deal of other information is contained in the text.

IR 9+

P. BUDDEE

44   The Escape of the Fenians

Longmans, 1972. o.p. 0 5821 5015 9 (Australia 1971)

Set in Fremantle in 1875 and based on the true story of the escape of six Fenian prisoners with the help of John Collins. Told in the first person by a boy who helps, this is an exciting adventure story in its own right and interesting as a piece of fiction about a little-known event.

IR 10+

Angela BULL

45   Child of Ebenezer

Collins, 1974. o.p. 0 0018 4772 4

Grace, child of a follower of a strict religious sect in a northern mill town in the 1880s, is befriended by an Irish family, but is witness to a wave of anti-Irish feeling. A picture of bigotry and violence emerge from this strange but readable novel.

IR 10+

46   Griselda

Collins, 1977. o.p. 0 0018 3723 0

Charlotte is passed from one governess to another by Aunt Jane when her parents go to America for a visit, and ends up at Winteredge, where she becomes friendly with Griselda, who is then disinherited, but they come together again. An unusual amd moral tale showing clearly the place of a Victorian child.

IR 9+

47   Treasure in the Fog
Illustrated by Joanna Worth
Collins, 1976. o.p. 0 0018 4819 4 (Collins Young Fiction)

Four children alone in a big house go to the circus in the fog and become involved in a mystery. A short, exciting story set in Victorian England, with strong characterization.

IR 8+

Melvin BURGESS

48   Burning Issy
Andersen, 1992. 0 8626 4381 3

Issy has a recurring nightmare of being burned. She is a stray child living with a man who helps people who are ill in seventeenth-century Lancashire. Her involvement with women who are thought to be witches shows how cruelly

From K.M. Peyton, *The Edge of the Cloud*

they were treated. A strange, confusing tale of the persecution of these women by men who did not understand.

IR 12+

Hester BURTON

49   Castors Away!
Illustrated by Victor Ambrus
Oxford, 1962. o.p.

An outstanding story of the Henchman family at the time of the Battle of Trafalgar, of their rescucitation of Sgt Bibb, of Tom and his part in the battle, of Edmund who follows in his father's footsteps as a doctor, and of Nell finding her woman's place in the scheme of things. Full of detail and period, but overwhelmingly a family story. The Suffolk countryside is beautifully depicted in Victor Ambrus's illustrations.

IR 10+

50   A Grenville Goes to Sea
Illustrated by Colin McNaughton
Heinemann, 1977. o.p. 4349 4926 4 (Long Ago Children)

A small gem of a story about Richard Grenville, off to sea at twelve years old to fight the French. Coming from a long line of seafarers, he is unwilling to admit his fear of heights, but conquers it and comes to love the life. The book culminates in the Battle of the Glorious First of June (Nelson against the French). Marred by ugly drawings, the book contains a wealth of detail about a boy's life as a midshipman in Nelson's navy.

IR 8+

51   The Henchmans at Home
Illustrated by Victor Ambrus
Oxford, 1970. o.p.

Six stories spanning eleven years giving good pictures of the life of a doctor's family with the three children growing up against the background of the Boer War. They are, however, rather unsatisfactory as the reader is left wanting more, but would read aloud well.

IR 9+

52 In Spite of All Terror
Oxford, 1968. o.p.

A moving, and at times harrowing, picture of England during the Second World War, especially of Dunkirk and the Battle of Britain, seen through the eyes of Liz, an orphan evacuee sent to a mill house in an Oxfordshire village. Out of her depth at the beginning, she finds the family she never had and comes to terms with herself. The differences in class and attitude are well drawn and the spirit of England at war is captured.

IR 10+

53 Kate Rider
Illustrated by Victor Ambrus
Oxford, 1974. o.p. 0 1927 1369 8

Kate tells of her family divided by the Civil War, her father a Parliamentarian and her brother a Royalist, and of the siege of Colchester with her father besieging his son inside. No side is taken and the tragedy of the war is clearly drawn. Kate is too young at first to go to court and has to find her own place. An outstanding story, enhanced by the illustrations by Victor Ambrus.

IR 10+

54 No Beat of Drum
Illustrated by Victor Ambrus
Oxford, 1966. o.p.

A fine, sombre story of an agricultural labourer sent to Van Diemen's Land in 1830 for his part in a demonstration which tried to get better wages for the labourers hit by the arrival of the threshing machine. Harsh reality prevails, although the story is not all black and white.

IR 10+

55   Otmoor for Ever!
Illustrations by Gareth Floyd
Hamilton, 1968. o.p. 0 2410 1611 8 (Antelope)

Based on the riot of Otmoor in 1830 when villagers cut down the fences which land owners had placed round the common land. Jake helps to save his brother Seth from gaol but cannot prevent the land from being fenced. This is a difficult subject to understand for the young reader at whom this series is aimed, but it would read aloud well to an older age group.

IR 9+

56   The Rebel
Illustrated by Victor Ambrus
Oxford, 1971. o.p. 0 1927 1334 5

An understanding portrayal of Stephen, an idealist caught up in the revolutionary fervour sweeping Europe and especially France. He goes to France to take part in this glorious event but finds that revolution has its dirty side and is thrown into prison. This experience scars him mentally and he returns home, beaten and disillusioned, to be nursed back to health, and to try out his ideals in a slum school. The story requires some maturity because of the political ideals espoused.

IR 13+

57   Riders of the Storm
Illustrated by Victor Ambrus
Oxford, 1972. o.p. 0 1927 1345 0

This continues the story of *The Rebel* in which Stephen goes to Manchester to teach, and meets Lucy Winter and her radical uncle. Stephen's ideals make him a champion of Benjamin Winter, and the group of radical friends find themselves in court, accused of sedition. A complex and difficult novel, requiring some understanding of political thought, but a marvellous book for the right reader.

IR 14+

58   **Thomas**
Illustrated by Victor Ambrus
Oxford, 1969. o.p.

A long and detailed story of three people whose lives are intertwined against the background of Cromwell's last years and the Restoration of the Monarchy. Thomas and Richenda marry, and Richard becomes a doctor. Their friendship is tested by the couple's conversion to the Quaker religion, but the Plague brings them all together. A deeply satisfying story demanding much of the reader in the understanding of the political and religious background.

IR 14+

59   **Through the Fire**
Line drawings by Gareth Floyd
Hamilton, 1969. o.p. (Antelope)

A brief story of two children who come with their father to London in 1666 to give succour to fellow Quakers in prison. Thomas is imprisoned, and his children witness the Fire of London and are instrumental in rescuing him and other prisoners. An exciting and adventurous story with serious undertones, and with good illustrations.

IR 7+

60   **Tim at Fur Fort**
Illustrated by Victor Ambrus
Hamilton, 1977. o.p. 0 2418 9571 5 (Antelope)

Tim has gone to Canada to work for the Hudson Bay Company. In 1822 the fort is struck by smallpox and he sets out with his employer's son to fetch help. An exciting story, full of detail, and a good portrait of a boy facing a testing time.

IR 8+

61   Time of Trial
Illustrated by Victor Ambrus
Oxford, 1963. o.p. (Carnegie Medal 1963)

Margaret's father, a bookseller, is imprisoned for putting his ideals in a pamphlet he published, and his bookshop is burned. Margaret goes to a small Suffolk fishing village to be near her father in Ipswich gaol, where she finds her fiancé's father is against her marrying Robert, and that the village is caught up in smuggling. A perfectly rounded story set against the background of the growth of ideas of men like Thomas Paine.

IR 12+

62   To Ravensrigg
Oxford, 1976. o.p. 0 1927 1393 0

In an England whose conscience is burdened by the slave trade, Emmie loses her father in a shipwreck and is rescued by a clergyman who is tortured by his past. Her father's dying words were to go to Ravensrigg and the quest for this house brings her into the company of a young Quaker with whom she falls in love. Told with Hester Burton's customary skill, although lacking the warmth of some of the other stories, but Emmie is a heroine in the Burton mould.

IR 12+

63   When the Beacons Blazed
Illustrated by Victor Ambrus
Hamilton, 1978. o.p. 0 2418 9837 4 (Antelope)

Kit Bassett and Nick Hawkins bring ammunition to the English fleet, meet Sir Francis Drake and ride to Dartmouth in a captured Spanish galleon. Full of details of Elizabethan life and capturing a boy's restlessness in the face of adventure. Would read aloud extremely well.

IR 7+

Helen BUSH

64 Mary Anning's Treasures
Illustrated by Gwyneth Cole
Gollancz, 1967. o.p.

Based on the true story of Mary Anning who aged twelve, discovered the skeleton of Ichthyosaurus in the cliffs of Lyme Regis, Dorset. She is introduced to fossil collecting by her father, who dies early on, and she carries on his work, collecting and selling, and supports her family. An interesting and unusual story with an index and a bibliography. Good for the fossil minded and for projects on fossils or dinosaurs.

IR 9+

Phyllis CALVERT

65 The Snowbird
Macmillan 1983. o.p. 0 3333 4249 6

In 1883 an orphaned brother and sister travel to Dakota from Tennessee to live with an uncle and aunt. On their arrival they witness the birth of the Snowbird, a white colt, and then settle down to life on the homestead. Tragedy strikes when Aunt Bella loses her baby, lets the Snowbird go, and leaves, but this spurs Wilianne to write again – this story. A moving story of a girl coming to terms with her dreams.

IR 10+

Bruce CARTER

66   B Flight
Hamilton, 1970. o.p. 0 2410 1834 X (Pseudonym for Richard Hough)

Will joins the Royal Flying Corps although under age, having been spurned by Vicky for losing the Junior Guides Race on the Lake District fells. His training is hard and short and he joins B Flight in France in 1917. A great deal of technical detail and a vivid picture of the Royal Flying Corps at war make this a book likely to appeal to less academic boys.

IR 10+

67   Peril on the Iron Road
Illustrated by Charlotte Hough
Hamilton, 1965. o.p. (Big Reindeer)

A technically detailed adventure story about the building of the railway from London to Birmingham and specifically a tunnel near Watford. George and Jimmy befriend a navvy, then help to rescue him from an explosion and end up by crashing a train into a blockage in the tunnel. This book would have benefited greatly from a map and some diagrams.

IR 9+

Peter CARTER

68   The Black Lamp
Illustrated by David Harris
Oxford, 1973. o.p. 0 1927 1356 6
Oxford, 1984. 0 1927 1497 X (Archway)

Daniel becomes an engineer, but marches with the weavers from his village to ask for suffrage at Peterloo. His father is wounded in the fighting and Daniel is helped to escape by one of the brotherhood of the Black Lamp. Eventually he rescues his sister from the children's dormitory at the mill and escapes to Yorkshire. A stark and grim story of man's fear of machines and his fight for his rights, unrelieved by much warmth.

IR 10+

69 Leaving Cheyenne
Oxford, 1990. 0 1927 1572 0

A large book, physically and in scope, this tells of Ben Curtis, whose brother is shot and who is left alone to fend for himself in the Midwest of America in the 1860s. He learns in a hard school, as a cowboy on the trail and in a primitive Dodge City. A real western, told in a suitably laconic style.

IR 14+

70 Madatan
Illustrated by Victor Ambrus
Oxford, 1974. o.p.
Oxford, 1987. 0 1927 1577 1 (Archway)

A powerful, stark and often violent story set at the end of the eighth century in which a boy, taken by the Norsemen, is found on the coast of Northumbria. Taken into the Church, he uses his wits and intelligence to make his way. A good picture of the early church finding its path between God and State, and of the warring factions in early England. The stark misery of life is a little hard to take and the book requires perseverance.

IR 12+

71 The Sentinels
Oxford, 1980. 0 1927 1433 4 (Guardian Award 1981)
R. Drew, 1987. 0 8626 7195 7 (Swallow)

A well researched and detailed indictment of the slave trade, telling the story of John Spencer, gentleman volunteeer at fifteen, on the Sentinel, bound for the anti-slave patrol off the west African coast. Told in phase with his story is that

From R. Sutcliff, *The Lantern Bearers*

of Lyabo, an African taken into slavery, his experiences on board the slave trader Phantom, and his friendship with John when they are marooned together. A fine picture of the Royal Navy of the day, of men in command and below decks, and of the appalling inhumanity of the slave trade. Many an adult would find this a rewarding read.

IR 14+

Winifred CAWLEY

72　Down the Long Stairs
Illustrated by William Stobbs
Oxford, 1964. o.p.

Set against the background of the Civil War in 1648. Ralph Cole, son of a Royalist is caught up in the battle of Tynemouth Castle and thereafter is on the run. Helped by miners (there is a good picture of the coal industry at the time) and by a Papist priest, he returns home, finds his vocation to be a doctor and flees to the continent. A pro-Royalist tinge does not spoil a good story.

IR 10+

73   The Feast of the Serpent
Illustrated by Doreen Roberts
Oxford, 1969. o.p. 0 1927 1309 4

Adonelle Heron rejects the ways of her mother's people, the Faa (gypsies), but finds a face from the past brands her as a witch. There is a horrifying picture of a witch's trial in the Puritan England of 1649, and for this it is worth persevering with this difficult story.

IR 10+

74   Gran at Coalgate
Illustrated by Fermin Rocker
Oxford, 1974. o.p. 0 1927 1366 3

Jinnie, (heroine of *Silver Everything*), studies too hard for the scholarship and is sent to recuperate with her Gran in a mining community in 1926. Here she finds that not everything her strict father has told her is true for example that dancing is sinful and widens her horizons. The Geordie accent makes for difficult reading, but this is a pleasant story of a girl growing up.

IR 10+

75   Silver Everything, and Many Mansions
Illustrated by William Stobbs
Oxford, 1976. o.p. 0 1927 1389 2

This book contains two long stories set in Tyneside in the 1920s. Jinnie, whose father is out of work, decides to take a shop in another part of town. She finds it hard to get on with the rougher new girls but eventually fits in. An interesting picture of life in the Depression emerges, with a great many small details. Would read aloud or dramatize well.

IR 9+

John CHRISTOPHER

76 Dom and Va
Hamilton, 1973. o.p. 0 2410 2329 7

Dom is a savage member of a tribe of hunters, befriended by a girl from a more civilized tribe of farmers who have used fire to cook and tools to carve. Dom and his tribe kill Va's people, but when Dom's father tries to take Va for himself Dom takes her and runs away. At first he tries to treat her as did the other men, but gradually this changes as he learns she will not love him like that. However, she continues to hate him until she and her son are threatened. An interesting and thought-provoking look at prehistoric man.

IR 12+

Richard CHURCH

77 The White Doe
Illustrated by John Ward
Heinemann, 1968. o.p. 1 4030 470 3

Tom Winter, the woodman's son, is friends with the Squire's son Billy on an estate in 1910. But Billy goes away to school and when the white doe Tom has seen is threatened by Harold, the bully, matters come to a head. A story of a friendship across the class structure of the time, with many descriptions of the countryside.

IR 9+

Joan CLARKE

78   Early Rising
Illustrated by Paulene Martin
Cape, 1974. o.p. 0 2240 1001 8

A gentle but perceptive story of a girl growing up in the 1860s. Erica is high spirited and under-confident, the middle child of five, who finds life difficult when her stepsister comes to take charge of the household. Country life with its class structure is clearly depicted as is the place of women at the time, for example, their lack of opportunity for education.

IR 10+

Pauline CLARKE

79   The Boy with the Erpingham Hood
Illustrated by Cecil Leslie
Faber, 1956. o.p.

A rather dated and slightly old-fashioned story which nevertheless captures the period well. This tells the story of a Norfolk boy who follows his lord to Agincourt and later becomes a mason. Some real characters from the time appear.

IR 10+

Elizabeth COATSWORTH

80   Away Goes Sally
Illustrated by Caroline Sharpe
Blackie, 1970. o.p. 0 2168 8618 X (USA 1934)

Sally and her family travel to Maine in a little house on runners on the snow. The first and the best of the books about Sally, not giving much detail of the harsher aspects of pioneer life in the eighteenth century, but a comfortable story for a young age group.

IR 8+

81 Five Bushel Farm
Illustrated by Caroline Sharpe
Blackie, 1970. o.p. 0 2168 7258 8 (USA 1939)

In the second of the series about Sally, Andrew, whose father is believed lost at sea, arrives in her warm and loving household. An episodic book, including the new house building, with many domestic details, but basically a family story of Andrew finding his niche.

IR 8+

82 The Fair American
Illustrated by Caroline Sharpe
Blackie, 1970. o.p. (USA 1940)

This, the third in the series, starts in France as Pierre an aristocratic boy flees from the Revolution. He is taken on as a cabin boy by Captain Patterson who has Sally and her family with him on a voyage from Maine. The voyage is eventful, but eventually they arrive safely and Pierre goes to his uncle in Boston. A lively story with some depth.

IR 9+

83 Here I Stay
Hamilton, 1972. o.p. 0 2410 2205 3 (USA 1938)

A calm, reflective story of a girl who stays on her father's farm in Maine after his death and also the departure of all their neighbours for new land in Ohio. It is a solitary life except for encounters with Indians and a young man. Beautiful descriptive passages of rural life give this book a timeless quality.

IR 12+

84 The Sailing Hatrack

Illustrated by Gavin Rowe
Blackie, 1972. o.p. 0 2168 9313 5 (USA 1951)

The *Sailing Hatrack* is a store-ship which plied along the coast of Maine in the late nineteenth century and is the background for a book full of details of the coastal villages and their life, and a sub-plot of two ne'er-do-wells who rescue the hero.

IR 10+

85 Sword of the Wilderness

Illustrated by Roger Payne
Blackie, 1972. o.p. 0 2168 7260 0 (USA 1936)

An account of a boy taken from his home on the Maine coast by Indians in 1689, and his life with them until he is rescued by his father the following year. Often stark and violent but in all a sympathetic view of Indian life and their differing treatment by the French and English settlers. The ending is sudden but right.

IR 9+

86 Tamar's Wager

Illustrated by Roger Payne
Blackie, 1971. o.p. 0 2168 8630 9 (USA title *The Golden Horseshoe*, 1935)

The half-Indian daughter of a Virginian gentleman, disguises herself as an Indian boy and with her white half-brother follows the Governor's expedition westwards from colonial Virginia. Her eventual return to her mother's people helps her to mature.

IR 10+

Marita CONLON-McKENNA

87   Under the Hawthorn Tree: Children of the Famine

Viking, 1991. 0 6708 3774 1 (Ireland, 1990)
(Winner of International Reading Association Award)

A sparingly written account of the experience of three children during the Great Famine between 1845–50 in Ireland,
who are evicted after the failure of their potato crop and
their father goes to search for work. Their mother goes to
look for him (a slightly implausible event) and the children,
after her non-return, go to find their aunts in Casteltaggart.
There are some horrifying details of starvation and illness.

IR 10+

Pam CONRAD

88   Prairie Songs

Oxford, 1987. 0 1927 1570 4
Puffin, 1989. 0 1403 2822 X (USA 1985)

In Nebraska in the ninteenth century, the coming of the
new doctor and his wife is a great event. Louisa admires
Emmeline, but she has come from the city and cannot adapt
to the soddy (dirt house) and the emptiness, and when she
loses her baby, her mind breaks. Louisa observes this tragedy and compares her mother with Emmeline. Stark, bare
prose for a tragic tale of pioneering life.

IR 12+

Catherine COOKSON

89   The Nipper

Illustrated by Tessa Jordan
Macdonald, 1970. o.p. 0 3560 3111 X
Puffin, 1973. 0 1403 0580 7

Sandy and his mother have to leave their tithe cottage and this means leaving the Galloway pony Sandy has trained from a foal. But he and Nipper meet up again when Sandy takes a job in the pit to be near him. Conditions underground in the Northumberland of the 1830s are appalling and the men strike under a moderate leader, although a more violent solution is foiled by Sandy and the Nipper. A readable story with a somewhat implausible ending, giving a good picture of mining at the time.

IR 10+

90 Rory's Fortune

Macdonald, 1988. 0 3561 1998 X (First published as *Blue Baccy* in 1972)

Rory is dragged into a smuggling network when he visits the West Country to fulfil his master's wish to visit his supposed mother. Interspersed with this adventure, the reader witnesses the grinding poverty of the Durham countryside in 1851. A good yarn written with Mrs Cookson's customary warmth and skill.

IR 10+

Gordon COOPER

91 A Certain Courage

Illustrated by Robin Jacques
Oxford, 1975. o.p. 0 1927 1375 2

A quiet story of an ordinary girl evacuated to an ordinary family at the outbreak of war in 1939, and how all their lives are touched by it. Hilary loses her grandmother, Mr and Mrs Collier their son, but the quiet domesticity of life goes on. It is difficult to explain to today's children what the life of an evacuee was like and this book goes a long way to describing it without any drama.

IR 9+

92   An Hour in the Morning
Illustrated by Philip Gough
Oxford, 1971. o.p.

Kate Bassett leaves school at twelve and goes into service
with Miss Nell Linden at Penrose Farm just before the Great
War. Nell is kind and Kate learns a lot, works hard and is
part of the secret of Nell's love for Sir Edward Carey. He is
killed during the war and when Nell's father dies, Kate and
Nell have to leave the farm. A deep, thoughtful book not
denying the hardship of the time.

IR 10+

93   A Time in the City
Illustrated by Robin Jacques
Oxford, 1972. o.p. 0 1927 134 1

Sequel to *An Hour in the Morning* telling of Kate's new
position as a kitchen maid in the Bourne household, thirty
miles away from her home. This means she cannot go home
often, but the friendship of the other maid and her family
eases the pain. Telling differences between her life and the
Bournes make this an interesting if uneventful story set in
the time of the Great War.

IR 10+

94   A Second Springtime
Illustrated by Robin Jacques
Oxford, 1973. 0 1292 7135 5

Hester Fielding, with her friend Bethanne and four other
orphans, travels to Nova Scotia from England to find a new
home in 1873. She is adopted by the Clarke family and, in
spite of the older son's hostility, settles down well. The
domestic and farming details of a homestead are well drawn.
There is tragedy at the end as Bethanne has not been so
fortunate, but this helps Hester's resolve to become a nurse.

IR 10+

95 Hester's Summer
Illustrated by Robin Jacques
Oxford, 1974. o.p. 0 1927 1361 2

Sequel to *A Second Springtime* in which Hester spends a year in the infirmary of the small town in Nova Scotia in 1880, training to be a district nurse. The small details of her life with the Clarke family, her friendships and the simple pleasures of life make a satisfying story.

IR 10+

Susan COOPER

96 Dawn of Fear
Illustrated by Margery Gill
Chatto, 1972. o.p. 0 7011 0484 8
Puffin, 1974. 0 1403 0719 2 (USA 1970)

Nightly air raids spent either in the garden shelter or under the Andersen shelter give a claustrophobic feel to the story of Peter, Derek and Geoff. They make a camp in the Ditch, and fight the local gang with the help of an older boy. There is a tragedy when Peter is killed in an air raid, and this is handled well in this exploration of relationships between the three boys.

IR 10+

Audrey COPPARD

97 Nancy of Nottingham
Heinemann, 1973. o.p. 4349 3302 3

Nancy moves to an aunt in Nottingham and works in the lace industry. Her growing awareness of social wrongs and her involvement in the Luddite movement are well drawn.

From R. Sutcliff, *The Lantern Bearers*

The reasons for the movement are clearly spelt out and a fair picture of the injustice emerges.

IR 10+

Gillian CROSS

98   The Iron Way
Oxford, 1979. o.p. 0 1927 1430 9
Oxford, 1990. 0 1927 1642 5 (Archway)

A quite outstanding novel depicting the effect of the building of the railway on a small Sussex village where the hostility between the navvies and the villagers flares into violence. Jem and his sister Kate take Con as a lodger, but find themselves cast out from the village. Kate, worn beyond her years, blossoms under Con's love but the violence takes him away from her.

IR 12+

Kevin CROSSLEY-HOLLAND

99   The Sea-Stranger
Illustrated by Joanna Troughton
Heinemann, 1973. o.p. 4 3494 9128 4 (Long Ago Children)

Wulf is the boy the Christian, Cedd, encounters on the beach in Essex in 653 AD, and who waits for his return.

There is an impressive description of the burial of a king (based on Sutton Hoo) and a feeling of the immensity of the arrival of Christianity in East Anglia.

IR 9+

100 The Fire-Brother
Illustrated by Joanna Troughton
Heinemann, 1975. o.p. 4349 4915 9 (Long Ago Children)

The second in the trilogy and the story of Oswald's attempt to destroy the monastery. A sense of calm and deep religious feeling pervades this book.

IR 9+

101 The Earth-Father
Illustrated by Joanna Troughton
Heinemann, 1976. o.p. 4349 4917 5 (Long Ago Children)

This concludes the trilogy and tells of Wulf's last meeting with Cedd, the Anglo-Saxon bishop, as he lies dying of the Plague at Lastingham. Cedd's death is drawn with dignity, not hiding anything, and this makes it a difficult topic for those for whom this book is intended. Beautifully written, it would read aloud well.

This trilogy is a tremendous achievement which needs to be used with children, read aloud or dramatized, but is an experience which should not be missed.

IR 9+

See also no. 409

Vera CUMBERLEGE

102 The Grey Apple Tree

Illustrated by Victor Ambrus
Deutsch, 1965. o.p. (Time, Place and Action)

An honest, and at times wooden, account of a Saxon village
at the time of the Battle of Hastings, and based on the
Domesday mention of Horsted. John runs away from his
Norman master to return to his grandfather's village, and
he and his cousin witness the horror of the battle. The
Normans are portrayed as rather bad masters, but their
influence is clearly seen.

IR 9+

Ruth DALLAS

103 Holiday Time in the Bush

Illustrated by Gary Hebley
Methuen, 1983. o.p. 0 416 23480 1

The small events in the life of a New Zealand family in
1891 – a pet show at school, Christmas, and a visit to the
seaside – make an attractive story for a younger age group.
It is well written with good characterization.

IR 7+

Marjorie DARKE

104 The First of Midnight

Illustrations by Anthony Morris
Kestrel, 1977. o.p. 0 7226 5304 2
Puffin, 1989. 0 1403 2770 3 (Plus)

A black slave is brought to Bristol and meets a white girl, a
slave in her own way, with whom he has an affair, before

he returns to Africa and she bears his child. It is written in dialect which makes for difficult reading and there is a fairly explicit sex scene. It paints a sordid picture of people who made their money from slaves, and provides an interesting look at life below stairs.

IR 14+

105   A Question of Courage
Illustrated by Janet Archer
Kestrel, 1975. o.p. 0 7226 5903 2
Armada, 1978. 0 0067 1212 6 (Lions)

A powerful and emotional story of a working-class girl from Birmingham and her unlikely friendship with a society girl, and how they get caught up in the Suffragette movement. The violence therein is well described, as is the position of women at the time; the social differences between the two girls are clearly underlined. Several well-known suffragettes appear in the story.

IR 12+

106   A Rose from Blighty
Collins, 1990. 0 0018 4686 8

The friendship between Emily and Louise from *A Question of Courage* is continued as the Great War means the Suffragette cause has to be set aside. Freedom comes in a different way with Emily training as a nurse and Louise involved in political canvassing. Emily's experiences as a nurse at the Front are well described.

IR 12+

107   Ride the Iron Horse
Decorations by Michael Jackson
Longmans, 1973. o.p. 0 5821 6030 8

The threat that the coming of engines, in particular the railway, posed to the agricultural worker, forms the plot of this book. John Gate is a farmworker, searching for a better life, hoping to find it through his friendship with the Squire's daughter (who helps him to read) and his work as a navvy on the railway. The ignorance and fear of change and unemployment are well drawn.

IR 12+

108 The Star Trap

Decorations by Michael Jackson
Longmans, 1974. o.p. 0 5821 6262 9

In the sequel to *Ride the Iron Horse*, Frances Redmayne's determination to become an actress makes for a detailed, if at times disjointed, picture of travelling theatre companies. Her romance with John Gate continues despite her father's disapproval of both this and her acting career.

IR 12+

Evelyn DAVIES

109 Cam

Illustrated by Janet Duchesne
Hamilton, 1980. o.p. 0 2411 0406 8 (Antelope)

A slight story in the Antelope format of an orphan boy taken in by farm labourers in the 1860s. Small details of the hard life and the injustices encountered filter in through the story.

IR 7+

110 Run for Home

Illustrated by Jane Paton
Hamilton, 1974. o.p. 0 2410 2406 4 (Antelope)

A story of the early settlers in America, when an English boy reluctantly joins the wagon train. When at last his parents settle he finds an Indian friend who helps him to find really good land for their farm. A little glib but very readable, and the reader will have sympathy for the hero having to move.

IR 8+

Marguerite DE ANGELI

111 The Black Fox of Lorne
Worlds Work, 1959. o.p. (USA 1956)

Twin brothers sail with their father from Norway for England, but see him killed by treachery. When one of them is taken prisoner they use their likeness to advantage, wait their moment and take revenge. The Black Fox is the villain trying to betray the King, but justice is done. Running through the story is the strong Christianity of the Scots, moving and credible. It is written in a stately style which gives an old-fashioned flavour, but none the worse for that. Set in tenth-century Scotland.

IR 8+

112 The Door in the Wall
Worlds Work, 1959. o.p. (USA 1949, Newbery Medal 1950)

A lovingly created medieval world is the setting for a deep tale of a boy laid low by a disease which cripples his legs. His father is away at the war, his mother waiting on the Queen, but he is rescued by Brother Luke and taken to Sir Peter's castle where he was to have learned to become a knight. How Robin comes to terms with his disability and through his courage earns the King's thanks, makes a fine story told in a stylized prose which fits the period exactly.

IR 9+

Kathy Lynn EMERSON

113 Julia's Mending
Orchard, 1987. 1 872 13068 7
Collins, 1989. 0 0067 3393 X (Lions) (USA 1987)

Rebellious Julia is sent to stay with her cousins on their
farm in 1887. She hates it and them, but gradually mellows
and comes to like them and enjoy herself. Easy reading, full
of small details of American rural life of the time, based on
the author's grandfather's experiences.

IR 8+

Gertie EVENHUIS

114 What About Me?
Translated from the Dutch by Lance Salway
Illustrated by Ron Stenberg.
Kestrel, 1974. o.p. 0 7226 6047 2 (Netherlands 1970)

Dirk wants to be part of the Resistance to which his brother
Sebastian and his father belong, but is always told he is too
young. He determines on his own course of action and
saves a Jewish child. In the midst of the breathlessness of
the prose and the pace of the story, the stark truth and
horror of the war come through. Written for a younger age
than most books about the war.

IR 8+

Willi FAHRMANN

115 The Fear of the Wolves; The Story of an Exodus
Translated by Stella Humphries
Illustrated by Victor Ambrus
Oxford, 1973. o.p. 0 1927 1348 5 (Germany 1971)

A harrowing tale of a Prussian family's flight from the Russian army in 1944. Konrad and his family have largely escaped the war on their farm in east Prussia, but as the Russians advance they have to leave the farm and travel west. Konrad's mother gives birth and they have to stop for a while, all the time seemingly only one step ahead of the Russians. The journey ends in Berlin and safety. An interesting picture of the German side of the war and giving an insight into the plight of the refugee.

IR 10+

B. FAIRFAX- LUCY and Philippa PEARCE

116   The Children of the House
Illustrated by John Sergeant
Gollancz, 1989. 0 5750 4539 6
Gollancz, 1991. 0 5750 5082 9

The four children, Laura, Tom, Hugh and Margaret, live a sad and lonely existence in a big house before the Great War. Thrown very much together and befriended by the servants, the only riches they have are their strong relationships with each other. This is a fragmentary tale, adapted by Philippa Pearce from an adult story.

IR 9+

Penelope FARMER

117   August the Fourth
Illustrated by Joel Jordan
Heinemann, 1975. o.p. 4349 4914 0 (Long Ago Children)

A deep, sad story of a girl looking back from the death of her brother in the Great War, to 4th August, 1914, the day it all began, when she, her brother and two friends go off for a picnic. Over it all hangs the shadow of war. This requires some emotional maturity from the reader and thus is not for this series' intended readership, but would read aloud well to an older age group.

IR 10+

Edward FENTON

118 Duffy's rocks
Hamilton, 1974. o.p. 2418 9135 3

An Irish-American family in the Pittsburgh of the Great Depression provides the backdrop to a boy's search for his errant father, and his strong relationship with his grand-mother. The book gives an interesting portrait of immigrant groups, and the closeness of their family life.

IR 12+

Kathleen FIDLER

119 The Droving Lad
Canongate, 1989. 0 8624 1154 (Kelpie)

Ian Cameron, desperate to join his father and grandfather on the droving road in 1863, listens to his grandfather, Colin's, tale of how he had to take the cattle alone on the road in 1813. His difficulties, whom to trust, and his encounters on the way, make an adventure story well worth this reissue.

IR 10+

120 The Railway Runaways
Illustrated by Terry Gasbey
Blackie, 1977. o.p. 0 2169 0206 7

From H. Burton, *In Spite of All Terror*

> An appealing story of two children who run away, just for the day, to ride on the horse-drawn railway from Edinburgh to Dalkeith to see Queen Victoria. Nicely ended and told with warmth and humour.

IR 8+

Esther FORBES

121 Johnny Tremain: A Novel for Young and Old

Longmans, 1944. o.p. 5 8211 5076 0 (USA 1943, Newbery Medal 1944)

> Johnny is apprenticed to a silversmith in Boston in 1773, but an accident to his hand puts paid to that and he becomes involved in the Boston Tea Party and the American

War of Independence. This long and complex story shows quite clearly how a revolution grows, and the background to events is slowly filled in so that at the end the reader will feel he has a complete picture. A deeply satisfying novel which has not dated at all.

IR 10+

Antonia FOREST

122   The Player's Boy
Faber, 1970. o.p. 0 5710 9516 X

Nicholas Marlowe runs away from home with Kit (Christopher) Marlowe and after a series of adventures joins Will Shakespeare and Burbage's theatre company. A complex, detailed and absorbing picture of Elizabethan life peopled with real characters such as Southampton and Essex. This would provide good background reading for those studying Shakespeare's work. There are many quotations, and allusions to political events which are not always explained in the text.

IR 12+

123   The Players and the Rebels
Faber, 1971. o.p. 0 5710 9605 9

The sequel to *The Player's Boy*, follows Nicholas Marlowe's fortunes, his growth as an actor and his involvement as a minor spy in Lord Essex's rebellion. Full of detail which brings the period vividly to life, with superb characterization. Shakespeare's work is liberally quoted, which sent this reader back to the plays and sonnets. A demanding read which is well worth the trouble.

IR 12+

Paula FOX

124 The Slave Dancer: A Novel
With illustrations by Eros Keith
Macmillan, 1974. o.p. 3331 6645 0
Macmillan, 1979. 0 3332 6008 2
(USA 1973, Newbery Medal, 1974)

Jessie, a Creole boy, is taken in New Orleans to be a ship's
boy on a slaver bound for Africa. It is crewed by villains,
except for Purvis, who in his rough way looks out for the
boy. Jessie escapes a shipwreck with a young black slave
and then makes his way back home, but the experience has
scarred him for life. All this is told in a series of economi-
cally worded episodes, painting an all the more horrific
picture of the conditions in which the slaves were kept.

IR 10+

Jean FRITZ

125 Brady
Penguin, 1971. o.p. (USA 1960)

In the Pennsylvania of 1836, Brady, son of a farmer/preacher,
finds keeping his mouth shut difficult, and is truly tested
when he discovers his father is part of the underground
railway to Canada for escaping slaves. In an exciting story
which seems simple and grows more complex as Brady
must have seen it, he sees a slave well on his way.

IR 10+

J. G. FYSON

126 Friend Fire and the Dark Wings
Illustrated by Annabel Large
Oxford, 1983. o.p. 0 1927 1467 8
Oxford, 1986. 0 1927 1539 9 (Archway)

One of the Wise Animals, an early tribe, discovers fire by
accident. It keeps him safe but he destroys his habitat with
it, so has to move in with his family. He discovers other
members of the tribe have also found Friend Fire. A rather
strange book with an annoying tweeness in the vocabulary,
but which gives an interesting look at very early man.

IR 9+

127 The Three Brothers of Ur
Illustrated by Victor Ambrus
Oxford, 1964. o.p.

Shamashazin is the eldest in a family who live in Ur nearly
four thousand years ago. Haran is the youngest, Nayckor
the middle child, and there are two sisters as well. Haran
befriends a donkey boy who is a clay modeller and helps
Haran when he breaks the Terapim, the household image,
while their father is away. A vivid story of family life, this
is a book for the few, but rewarding for them.

IR 10+

128 Journey of the Eldest Son
Illustrated by Victor Ambrus
Oxford, 1965. o.p.

In this sequel to *The Three Brothers of Ur*, Shamashazin sets
out on the caravan, is hurt, nursed back to health, and finds
his true faith. This is the story of Abraham under another
name, a remarkably convincing reconstruction of life four
thousand years ago.

IR 12+

Jane GARDAM

129 A Few Fair Days

Julia McRae, 1987. 0 8620 3302 0

Walker, 1989. 0 7445 1337 5

Glimpses of Lucy and her childhood in the 1930s are given in separate stories that tell of her relationship with the aunts and her grandmother, and her best friend Mary. Beautifully written, this would read aloud well.

IR 8+

Leon GARFIELD

130 Smith

Illustrated by Anthony Maitland

Longmans, 1967. o.p.

Puffin, 1968. 0 1403 0340 8

In this Dickensian tale, Smith takes a document from a man later killed and finds this leads him into trouble. He befriends a blind magistrate but is then thrown into Newgate Gaol. An array of suitably seedy characters inhabit this twilight world, and it is only Smith to whom the reader warms. It is beautifully written by a man whose books refuse to be categorized.

IR 10+

Alan GARNER

The Stone Book Quartet

Collins, 1983. 0 0018 4282 X

This comprises four separate books, each telling of an episode in the lives of a family of Cheshire craftsmen at four points in history, 1864, 1886, 1916 and 1941. Beautifully written, all these stories would benefit greatly from being read aloud, making them a shared experience. They are, in order:

131 The Stone Book
Etchings by Michael Foreman
Collins, 1976. o.p. 0 0018 4777 5

Mary takes lunch to her father working on the church tower and expresses the desire for a book, although she cannot read. Her father's answer is to take her into the hillside to see a marvellous secret, an ancient cave painting, and then he makes her a stone book.

IR 9+

132 Granny Reardun
Etchings by Michael Foreman
Collins, 1977. 0 0018 4288 9

Joseph watches a stone house being pulled down and his grandfather using the stone to make a wall. He knows, however, that this is not what he wants to do, and he summons up the courage to become apprenticed to a blacksmith. To his surprise his grandfather agrees.

IR 9+

133 The Aimer Gate
Etchings by Michael Foreman
Collins, 1978. 0 0018 4067 3

Robert reaches his secret place in the church tower (which Mary's grandfather built) to find *his* grandfather's mark, finds out what Charlie does while he's home on leave from the Great War, and helps in the cutting of the corn. All these small episodes make a picture of seemingly unimportant moments.

IR 9+

134 Tom Fobble's Day
Etchings by Michael Foreman
Collins, 1977. 0 0018 4832 1

William's grandfather, Joseph, makes him a proper sledge after Stewart had 'Tom Fobbled' it. William sledges at night during an air raid, returning to find his grandfather dying.

IR 9+

Maurice GEE

135 The Champion
Puffin, 1989. 0 1403 4160 9

Rex's mother takes in a wounded American soldier, but he is not the heroic figure Rex expected, worse he admits to being afraid of fighting. Gradually Rex comes to see that war is fought by ordinary men. There is a tragic ending to this story set in New Zealand in 1943.

IR 10+

Adele GERAS

136 Voyage
Hamilton, 1983. o.p. 0 2411 0988 4
Armada, 1985. 0 0067 2409 4 (Lions)

A sad, haunting story of Jewish passengers in the steerage section of S.S. Danzig as it sails from Europe to America in 1904. The past is mingled with the present, although two love stories form the central theme, and behind them all is the sadness of a persecuted race.

IR 12+

Griselda GIFFORD

137 The Story of Ranald
Illustrated by Edward Gage
Bodley Head, 1968. o.p.
Canongate, 1985. 0 8624 1094 0 (Kelpie)

After the Battle of Culloden, Randald Macdonald and his stepmother and sisters, flee their home. Eventually he ends up in England. His father is sentenced to death for his part in the uprising. This is a moving story based on Ranald's own account written in 1749.

IR 9+

Barbara GILES

138 Bill
Puffin, 1988. o.p. 0 1403 2553 0

A slight, readable story of Bill, sent to live with his unknown curmudgeonly grandfather in the outback of Australia in 1934 while his mother is ill and his father is away looking for work. He finds the old man difficult but makes friends and settles down although he worries about his mother. He saves his grandfather's life and a family reconciliation ends the story.

IR 8+

Bill GILLHAM

139 Home Before Long
Illustrated by Francis Mosley
Deutsch, 1983. 0 2339 7561 6

Bill and Dorothy (six and nine respectively) are evacuated to Dorset, but do not find Mrs Updike to their liking so

Dorothy decides they will return to their mother in London. Their journey is exciting and they are helped along, but at the journey's end there is a shock. Dorothy's sturdy courage and the wartime atmosphere are well drawn.

IR 8+

Harriet GRAHAM

140 Frances and the Queen's Golden Angel
Illustrated by Geoffrey Bargery
Hamilton, 1976. o.p. 0 2418 9318 6 (Antelope)

Set in 1702, this tells of Frances Morton who longed to see Queen Anne but fell ill just before the wedding the Queen was to attend, and how her wish was fulfilled. It is beautifully written and a story to appeal to all small girls.

IR 7+

Bette GREENE

141 Summer of My German Soldier
Hamilton, 1974. o.p. 2418 9136 1
Puffin, 1988. 0 1403 2726 6 (Plus) (USA 1973)

Patty Bergen befriends a German POW on the run and shelters him, largely because he cares for her while her truly awful parents do not. When Anton is shot resisting arrest, Patty is convicted and sent to a reformatory. Patty only copes because of Anton's friendship and the support of the coloured maid. This is an emotional and telling picture of small-town America caught in fear during the Second World War.

IR 12+

Frederick GRICE

142 Aidan and the Strollers
Illustrated by William Stobbs
Cape, 1960. o.p.

A dramatic opening starts this adventure off well and a fast
pace keeps the reader involved. Aidan runs away from his
uncle's home and by chance encounters a group of strolling
players. He makes a good friend and they have a series of
adventures on their way to London. Edmund Kean makes
a brief appearance, and a liberal spattering of Shakespear-
ean quotations keeps the theatrical atmosphere alive.

IR 10+

143 The Black Hand Gang
Illustrated by Doreen Roberts
Oxford, 1971. o.p. 0 1927 1327 2

Set at the end of the Great War, this slight tale is about
Colin, whose father is a prisoner of war, and who is finding
life hard. There are even women teachers at school! The
gang of the title form a sub-plot in an episodic book illus-
trating working-class life at this time.

IR 7+

144 The Bonnie Pit Laddie
Illustrated by Brian Wildsmith
Oxford, 1960. o.p.
Puffin, 1980. 0 1403 1190 4

Richard Ullathorne sees a miners' strike reduce a small pit
community to its knees in northern England in the 1920s.
The men are forced back to work and then, only a year
later, hit by a disaster which, thanks to the courage of
Richard and his brother, has a happy ending. A tough un-
compromising, but human story of a boy striving for something, he knows not what.

IR 10+

From L.I. Wilder, *By the Shores of Silver Lake*

145   The Courage of Andy Robson
Oxford, 1969. o.p.

Andy is sent to Northumbria from his Tyneside pit village after his father has an accident. His adjustment to country life and his growing awareness of the fact that this is where he wishes to live are well drawn. He is determined to beat the bully, Billy, at wrestling, and to help his uncle protect the famed herd of cattle. This is the best of Grice's work, being a complete story rather than a series of linked episodes.

IR 9+

146   Nine Days' Wonder
Illustrated by Paul Ritchie
Oxford, 1976. o.p.

The nine days of the title are the days of the General Strike in 1926, observed by the son of a striking miner in a Durham pit, who questions his own values after observing the strike. The hardship of the miners' struggle is told in understated prose, which nevertheless is very moving. Told very much from the union side.

IR 10+

147   Young Tom Sawbones
Illustrated by Ian Ribbons
Oxford, 1972. o.p. 0 1927 1339 6

Tom Sawbridge, son of a doctor, follows his father north to his work among the railway navvies building the line between Yorkshire and Lancashire in the 1840s. A vivid picture is drawn of the nomadic navvies and their appalling working and living conditions, and of the growth of Tom's vocation to be a doctor like his father. The dialect makes it a little difficult to read sometimes and the illustrations are very smudgy.

IR 10+

Helen GRIFFITHS

148 The Kershaw Dogs
Illustrated by Douglas Hare
Hutchinson, 1976. o.p. 0 0913 2840 3

Dudley lives with his father in a stone pub, on a bleak
Yorkshire moor in the 1930s. He is lonely and unloved until
his father allows him to choose a pup to train and take part
in dogfighting, at that time an illegal sport, but still carried
out. The dog, Grip, loves Dudley and the boy learns to love
him. An interesting story with an unusual slant.

IR 9+

149 Witch Fear
Illustrated by Victor Ambrus
Hutchinson, 1975. o.p. 0 0912 4600 8

Into an unnamed village somewhere in Europe in 1540,
comes a small girl called Agnes, unwilling to speak. She is
taken in by Klaus and Wilhemina in place of their daughter
who died. Agnes only comes to life when playing with a
cat she has rescued, but a cat at this time was a familiar of
witches and the child is accused of being a witch. In fact
Agnes is autistic, and only common sense and a man's
discovery of the truth saves her. A chilling story of ignorance and fear.

IR 12+

Claude GUTMAN

150 The Empty House
Translated from the French by Anthea Bell
Turton & Chambers, 1991. 1 8721 4845 X
(France, 1989. Prix Sorcières, Best Young People's Novel.)

David and his parents have fled to Paris after a pogrom in
their native Poland. David is protected by friendly neigh-

bours, then a Catholic school and a refuge for Jewish children, as the Nazis round up the Jews. His Jewishness becomes all the more important to him, the more it is threatened. It is written in stark, spare prose, much as it happened, and is a moving experience.

IR 12+

151 Fighting Back
Translated from the French by Anthea Bell
Turton & Chambers, 1992. 1 8721 48875 1 (France, 1991)

The second part of a planned trilogy. David (of *The Empty House*) joins the Maquis and takes part in the liberation of France, only to find at the end of the book that his parents have been killed. A stark and moving story.

IR 12+

Dennis HAMLEY

152 Very Far From Here
Deutsch, 1976. o.p. 0 2339 6755 9

Eddy is caught up in the anti-German hysteria at the start of the Great War, and filled with ideas by Mrs Foskett, who is convinced the Germans will invade. Eddy 'finds' a spy in Mr Brown with his bicycle shop and a friend with a German car. It all goes horribly wrong when the mob gets carried away, but Mr Brown is remarkably forgiving and Eddy learns a valuable lesson. A plausible story with more than a touch of humour.

IR 10+

153 The War and Freddy
Illustrated by George Buchanan
Deutsch, 1991. 0 2339 8662 6
Deutsch, 1991. 0 2339 8756 8

Freddy is three in 1939, and nine when the war ends, and these stories told with humour cover those years. War starts as a game for him but slowly, and particularly when his father is called up, Freddy realizes the reality of it all. A small boy's perception of war as it affected him, ending happily with his father's return, beautifully illustrated by George Buchanan.

IR 7+

Cynthia HARNETT

154 The Great House
Illustrated by the author
Methuen, 1949. 0 4165 1220 8

The father of Barbara and Geoffrey plans to build a great house near Oxford in the 1690s but this is delayed and the two are left at the site, while he returns to London. Geoffrey desires above all to be an architect and, using his father's plans, maps out the site. The wealth of domestic detail in the text is illustrated by Cynthia Harnett's drawings and makes the period live for the reader.

IR 10+

155 The Load of Unicorn
Illustrated by the author
Methuen, 1959. o.p.

The unicorn is the watermark on the paper that Bendy's brothers try to prevent William Caxton from having: part of the battle the scriveners were having with the new fangled printers. This is an exciting and detailed story of a boy's involvement in a fight against change. It is not an easy read, but the depth and warmth of the characterization make it a rewarding experience.

IR 10+

156 Ring out Bow Bells!
Illustrated by the author
Methuen, 1953. 0 4165 4770 2

The setting is London at the time of Agincourt, where Dickon is apprenticed to Whittington, a mercer. Unwittingly he becomes involved in a Lollard plot, but all ends well at the battle of Agincourt. The wealth of detail, lovingly illustrated on almost every page, makes this a rewarding read, but it does require perseverance if the young reader is not to be submerged beneath it all.

IR 10+

157 Stars of Fortune
Illustrated by the author
Methuen, 1956. o.p. 0 4168 9880

A fascinating and detailed picture of life in the large Washington family caught up in the drama surrounding the Lady Elizabeth (captive at Woodstock) and a plot to free her. This story is based on an actual family and it is the details of family life which make for a satisfying, if somewhat dated, book.

IR 10+

158 The Wool-Pack
Methuen, 1951. o.p. (Carnegie Medal 1951)
Puffin, n.d. 0 1403 0153 4

Nicholas, a member of a Cotswold wool family, is instrumental in saving his father from the Lombards. Set around 1492 (there is a mention of Christopher Columbus), this book gives a tremendous amount of detail about life in the late fifteenth century, but the reader will warm to the characters of Nicholas and Cecily, his betrothed.

IR 10+

159 The Writing on the Hearth
Illustrated by Gareth Floyd
Methuen, 1971. 0 4164 6760 1

A beautifully written and exciting story of Stephen's relationship with the Suffolk family at the time of Henry VI. Vivid details of life at the time, of politics, witchcraft and sorcery speed the story along. The characterization is deep and rounded and makes for a satisfying story. There is an interesting description of the growth of the Oxford colleges and the life of the gentry of the time. A postscript fills in the historical detail and includes a letter from Suffolk to his son.

IR 10+

Ruth Elwyn HARRIS

160   The Silent Shore
Julia MacRae, 1986. 0 8620 3239 3
Walker, I989. 0 7445 1313 8

Sarah Purcell is seven when her mother dies and she narrates her version of events. Mr Mckenzie supervises her education and Gabriel, his son, encourages her ambition to write. A well-written family story set in the Quantock hills between 1910 and 1920.

IR 12+

161   The Beckoning Hills
Julia MacRae, 1987. 0 8620 3326 8
Walker, 1989. 0 7445 1356 1

This is Frances's version of the years covered in *The Silent Shore*. She first meets the Rector's son at the reading of her mother's will. He aids her desire to go art school, and she eventually goes to the Slade. Various well-known artists appear briefly in the story.

IR 12+

162   The Dividing Sea
Julia MacRae, 1989. 0 8620 3370 5
Walker, 1990. 0 744 51757 5

This is Julia's story, concentrating on her (often harrowing) experiences as a nurse in the Great War, Geoffrey Mckenzie's death and her eventual romance with David. Each of these three titles stands alone, although it is obviously helpful to have read the other two.

IR 12+

E. HARTENSTEIN

163   Firelight the Red Stallion
Translated from the German by Rosaleen Ockenden
Bodley, 1970. o.p. 0 3700 1024 8

Hawkeye grows to manhood in a tribe of horse hunters and is trained to take over the tribe, but there is disagreement amongst them as to how to kill the horses, whether to annihilate the herd, or just take part of it. This is resolved slowly throughout the story. Alongside his story is that of Firelight, a foal when the book starts. An unusual and compelling story of early man.

IR 12+

Evert HARTMAN

164   War Without Friends
Chatto, 1982. o.p. 0 7011 2650 7 (Netherlands 1979)

Arnold, son of a member of the Dutch Nazi Party, at first toes the Party line, informing on his friends, and suffering the inevitable consequences at school. But he does come to understand that he is not told the truth about the Germans, and in a spectacular denouement helps a Resistance worker to escape. It is a powerful story not helped by the fact that Arnold is such an unpleasant young man.

IR 12+

Erick Christian HAUGAARD

165 Chase Me, Catch Nobody
Granada, 1982. o.p. 0 2461 1938 1

Erik is a Danish schoolboy on a trip to Germany in 1937, and on the ferry he takes a package from a stranger and promises to deliver it. This brings him into conflict with the Nazi regime and he runs away encountering a Jewish girl whom he helps to escape to Denmark. There is a slightly implausible ending, but the underlying terror of the situation comes through.

IR 10+

166 The Little Fishes
Illustrated by Milton Johnson
Gollancz, 1969. o.p. 0 575 0021 X

Guido, an orphan boy in Naples in 1944, befriends Anna and her brother Mario, and together they tramp across Italy making for Cassino, begging for food and money. Although they encounter kindness, Mario dies, and Guido and Luigi (another friend) go to the Allies for help. A sad story of refugees made all the more poignant by the fact that they were children.

IR 9+

Kathleen HERSOM

167 The Half Child
Simon and Schuster, 1989. 0 6716 5331 8
Simon and Schuster, 1990. 0 7500 0456 8 (Young Books)

When Lucy's little sister, the half child of the title disappears, she sets out to look for her to no avail. Her mother dies and her father remarries, and then, while in service, she hears of a child taken in. The wheel comes full circle when her step-sister gives birth to a child bearing the signs of Downs Syndrome. Set in northern England at the time of the Civil War, this unusual story, told in lovely prose full of the period and the countryside, is a magical experience.

IR 9+

168 The Spitting Image
Illustrated by Derek Collard
Macmillan, 1982. o.p. 0 3333 2852 3

Old Jacob the gargoyle remembers episodes viewed from his vantage point on the church in a village in the Yorkshire Dales. He reminisces about the Plague, the reivers, old riddles and so on, making this an interesting way of looking at local history. This would need using with children because it is not an immediately attractive book, but it does have a humour of its own.

IR 9+

Archie HILL

169 Dark Pastures
Macmillan, 1981. o.p. 0 3333 0692 9 (Topliner Trident)

A racy novel of a boy joining the canal cutters and becoming mixed up in the fight with the railway men which threatened to become a private war. Set in the early nineteenth century in the Midlands, it paints a rough, tough life

From H. Burton, *Castors Away!*

which is also full of human warmth and kindness, and gives a good idea of the working conditions of the time.

IR 12+

C. Walter HODGES

170 Columbus Sails
Illustrated by the author
Bell, 1939 o.p. 7135 0551 6

An extremely detailed account, told mostly from a sailor's viewpoint, of Columbus's first voyage in 1492 when he discovered the West Indies and Haiti. It is difficult to get into, but worth the trouble for the depth of the story and the way it brings the enormity of his task to the reader, something which is difficult for the modern child to comprehend. It would read aloud well and dramatize even better. Walter Hodges' own very black drawings suit the story perfectly.

IR 9+

171 The Namesake: A Story of King Alfred
Illustrated by the author
Bell, 1964. o.p. 0 7135 0553 2

The story of Alfred's early kingship and the welding together of Saxon Wessex against the Danes, as seen through the eyes of his namesake, a crippled boy. Life is seen as bleak, with survival the main necessity. Alfred's style of kingship, quite different from that of his predecessors, is clearly drawn, as is the hold which Christianity had over the early Saxons. A marvellous story to read which does need perseverance.

IR 12+

172 The Marsh King

Bell, 1967. 0 1735 0552 4

This powerful sequel to *The Namesake* tells of Alfred's conquering of Guthorn, the Dane who became King Athelstan. Written in a stark prose befitting the saga-like nature of the story with its many bloody battles, but with a little warmth here and there particularly in Alfred's treatment of children and his people. He emerges as a wise king and, although not a hero in the Sutcliff mould, dominates in a quiet way. A version of how he burnt the cakes is included. There are two useful maps.

IR 12+

173 The Overland Launch

Illustrated by the author
Bell, 1969. o.p. 0 7135 1546 5

A fictionalized account (with some additional characters) of how the Lynmouth lifeboat was pulled across the moor to Porlock to help a boat in distress when it was impossible to launch the boat at Lynmouth. It is very detailed in its description of the physical task, but is not without humour. It would need introduction but be useful for project work on the sea, etc.

IR 10+

174 Playhouse Tales

Illustrated by the author
Bell, 1974. o.p. 0 7135 1819 7

A series of attactively presented tales of Elizabethan theatre life featuring figures such as Ben Jonson, Shakespeare, the Burbages, and Will Kemp, which are full of life and character.

IR 10+

Jacynth HOPE-SIMPSON

175 The Gunner's Boy
Heinemann, 1973. o.p. 4349 4315 0

In Elizabethan England, Mark is mistaken for his brother and hauled aboard Grenville's ship *The Revenge* at Plymouth, eventually becoming the gunner's boy. The excitement and tragedy of war, and the companionship of shipboard life are well described in this well-paced book.

IR 9+

176 The Ice Fair
Illustrated by Pat Marriott
Hamilton, 1963. o.p. 2419 0273 8 (Reindeer)

A vivid and exciting story in which a boy staying in London in the latter part of the seventeenth century when the Thames froze over, overhears a plot to blow up London Bridge. He and Margery enlist the help of the Hob and the Blackguards to rescue King Charles II.

IR 8+

177 The Unknown Island
Hamilton, 1968. o.p. 2419 1417 5

Philip goes to Syracuse in Sicily to seek his father who is a prisoner after the defeat of the Athenians. He meets with Rusty, a former slave, and although Rusty's worship of another goddess disturbs Philip's belief in the superiority of the Athenians, they work together to rescue Philip's father from the appalling conditions of the quarries, and begin to make their way home. A rewarding book which deserves to be better known and one of the few able to make the ancient past come alive.

IR 9+

178 Vote for Victoria
Illustrated by Joel Jordan
Heinemann, 1976. o.p. 4349 4920 5 (Long Ago Children)

Based on fact, this tells of Victoria and Dodo's experiences when caught up in the Suffragette movement, in particular how Victoria hid in the organ loft at a public meeting and of their attendance at a rally at the Albert Hall. The iniquitous position of women at the time is clearly drawn and, although the topic is difficult for those for whom this book is intended, it could well be read aloud to older children.

IR 10+

Dorothy HORGAN

179 The Edge of War
Oxford, 1987. 0 1927 1574 7
Oxford, 1991. 0 1927 1666 2

Anna, a German Catholic, sees her father taken away and court-martialled and then sent to a mental hospital for his resistance to the Nazis. Her search for him and her fight for survival form the story which is a little glib in parts but which shows what happened to a family who resisted Hitler.

IR 10+

Ellen HOWARD

180 Edith Herself
Collins, 1988. 0 0018 4254 4

After her mother's death Edith goes to live with her married sister, whose husband is a strict Christian and a schoolmaster. The strain seems to bring on fits and she has to learn to cope with these. Unexpectedly her help comes from

John, the husband, and his encouragement and determination that she shall lead a normal life, enable her to carry on. There is little detail of the epilepsy, but much incidental information about the way of life in the America of the 1890s.

IR 8+

Janni HOWKER

181 Isaac Campion
Julia MacRae, 1986. 0 8620 3270 9
Armada, 1987. 0 0067 2790 5 (Lions)

Isaac, as an old man, looks back to the day in 1901 when his brother Dan, his father's favourite, was killed in a dare by the son of his father's great enemy. Isaac has to leave school to help in his father's stables and his uncles are called on to help perpetuate the feud. There is very little love or warmth in this raw story, just the will to live and succeed, but it is a worthwhile experience nevertheless.

IR 12+

Irene HUNT

182 Across Five Aprils
Bodley, 1965. o.p. 3 7000 9950 9 (USA 1964)

The American Civil War is seen through the eyes of an Illinois farming family sitting at home waiting for letters from the front. These letters, difficult to read at times because they are reproduced in the dialect of the time, show clearly the muddle of war. An interesting piece appears at the end when Jeth's brother-in-law wonders if Lincoln's 13th Amendment will change the position of coloured men.

IR 14+

Mollie HUNTER

183 The Ghosts of Glencoe
Evans, 1966. o.p.

The story of the massacre of the Macdonalds at Glencoe by the soldiers of the Campbell regiment, the Argylls, told by Ensign Robert Stewart, who when told of the plan warned some of them and escaped himself. Based on a story in existence of such a deed, this powerful and moving tale, set in the magnificent scenery of the Highlands is vividly told.

IR 12+

184 A Pistol in the Greenyards
Illustrated by Elizabeth Grant
Evans, 1965. o.p.
Canongate, 1988. 0 8624 175 0 (Kelpie)

The tenants of farms in a Scottish glen are evicted so that the land can be sold for sheep grazing. Their resistance brings savage punishment and a massacre. The story is told in swift moving and stirring prose, with just the rhythm of the words giving the sound of the dialect, and is based on historical fact.

IR 12+

185 The Spanish Letters
Illustrated by Elizabeth Grant
Evans, 1964. o.p.
Canongate, 1984. 0 8624 1057 6

The hero is a 'Caddie', a member of a strange brotherhood in Edinburgh, who aids an English spy and a Scottish swordsman to foil a plot by Philip of Spain to overthrow King James Stuart and thus hurt Elizabeth I. Parts of this yarn are slightly implausible, but the pace carries the reader with it, and the confused background of the time is competently explained.

IR 10+

186 The Stronghold

Hamilton, 1974. 2418 9026 8 (Carnegie Medal 1974)

An outstanding reconstruction of how the broch (the strong-hold of the title) which appears only in the Orkneys, might have come to be. The hero, a crippled young member of an early tribe, finds his distinction not in the traditional war-rior field, but in the design of the stronghold which saves his tribe from the Roman invaders. The hold of the old religion of the Druids is powerfully described and the sac-rificial scene is a high point in the story.

IR 12+

187 You Never Knew Her as I Did

Hamilton, 1985. o.p. 0 2411 0643 5

A romantic and exciting re-enactment of one of the many dramas in the life of Mary, Queen of Scots; her imprison-ment in Lochleven Castle and her eventual escape in the guise of a soldier's wife. Will Douglas, bastard son of William Douglas the Master of Lochleven, tells the story, caught by the spell which Mary so obviously wove around those who met her. Mary is richly drawn and it is easy to see from this story why she was so followed and also so hated.

IR 10+

Annabel and Edgar JOHNSON

188 Torrie

Illustrated by Pearl Falconer
Brockhampton, 1961. o.p. (USA 1960)

Thomas Anders takes his family in a wagon across America from St Louis to settle in California. During this journey their daughter Torrie grows up and falls in love with Jess, an illiterate boy who joins them. The hardships which came

from lack of food and water, and the quarrelling between
the settlers are well described.

IR 10+

Carol JONES

189 The Painted Boats
Hamilton, 1979. o.p. 0 2411 0294 4

Told in retrospect, this story is of a boy growing up on the
canal boats in the 1900s, written so that the reader feels Ben
is beside him. The family is separated by circumstance, and
Ben grows up alone.

IR 10+

Margaret JOWETT

190 A Cry of Players
Illustrated by Asgeir Scott
Oxford, 1961. o.p.

Harry Lulworth, son of a player, finds the call of the theatre
impossible to resist. He joins Edward Alleyn and his company, touring England and returning to London when the
Plague and the City council let them. Harry plays the girls'
parts and the story ends with him triumphant as Juliet in
Shakespeare's play. A vibrant portrayal of the Elizabethan
theatre, with appearances by Shakespeare, Marlowe and
Alleyn.

IR 10+

191 Candidate for Fame
Illustrated by Peggy Fortnum
Oxford, 1955. o.p.

Many famous actors people the story of Deborah Keate, daughter of an actor manager in the time of George III. Showing great promise, she moves from York to Bath and thence to Sheridan's Drury Lane company. Full of literary and theatrical detail, this is alive with a girl's ambition to be an actress.

IR 10+

P.J. KAVANAGH

192 Scarf Jack
Bodley, 1978. o.p. 0 3703 0079 3
Puffin, 1980. 0 1403 1208 0

Francis rescues from hanging a man who is on the run from soldiers from Ireland led by Hunter Gowan. Gowan is eventually killed, although not by the man known as Scarf Jack, who turns out to be Francis' long lost father. Jack acknowledges him briefly before disappearing again. An adventure story which is set in Gloucestershire but with the background of the troubles in Ireland in 1789.

IR 10+

193 Rebel for Good
Bodley, 1980. o.p. 0 3703 0326 1

Sequel to *Scarf Jack* in which Francis follows his father's trail to the American West via a spell on an American Navy ship as assistant-surgeon, a journey with a French botanist, and a stay with a frontier man, before finally meeting his father with the Indian leaders. An exciting story in which Francis tests himself and learns about his father.

IR 10+

From R. Welch, *Captain of Foot*

Mara KAY

194 Storm Warning

Macmillan, 1976. o.p. 0 3331 8118 2
Goodchild, 1984. 0 8639 1048 3

Anna, an English girl travelling with her uncle in Germany
in 1938, stays with a widow and her son in Frankfurt after a
car accident. Frau Meixner is hiding two Jewish girls and
after her discovery of them Anna becomes involved in trying to help them escape. A frighteningly authentic picture
of Hitler's power in the last year before the Second World
War.

IR 10+

Harold KEITH

195 Komantcia

Illustrated by Charles Keeping
Oxford, 1966. o.p. 1927 1264 0 (USA 1965)

Pedro, an aristocratic Spanish boy, is taken by the Comanche
at fifteen, and used by them as a slave until a change of
ownership when he is trained as a warrior. The reader is
spared none of the violence, but it is an account fair to the
Indians, telling of the good and bad within them and their
way of life.

IR 14+

196 Rifles for Watie

Oxford, 1960. o.p. (USA 1957, Newbery Medal 1958)

Jeff, a Kansas farm boy, joins the Union army at the outbreak of the Civil War, full of fire and enthusiam. He encounters a twisted officer and a beautiful girl, and after a
career as infantryman, cavalryman and scout, joins Watie's
Rebels. This is a fine, detailed account of a boy, drawn into

war by his ideals, learning that it is not all black and white
and is full of action and camaraderie.

IR 12+

Judith KERR

197 When Hitler Stole Pink Rabbit
Illustrated by the author
Collins, 1971. 0 0018 4913 1
Armada, 1974. 0 0067 0801 3 (Lions)

Jewish Anna and her family leave Berlin in 1933 to escape
persecution, living first in Switzerland, then in France and
England. Papa is a famous journalist but finds it difficult to
get work so life is not easy. However, a strong family love
carries them through. The difficulties are not glossed over,
nor is the harshness of life in Nazi Germany.

IR 9+

198 The Other Way Round
Collins, 1975. o.p. 0 0018 4604 3
Collins, 1989. 0 0019 272 0

Sequel to *When Hitler Stole Pink Rabbit* which finds Anna
and her family in London at the outbreak of war. Life as
refugees is hard and they live from hand to mouth through
the Battle of Britain and the Blitz. But Anna finds she loves
to draw and paint and has talent. Glimpses of tragedy and
the awfulness of war do not obliterate the story of a girl
growing up.

IR 10+

Geoffrey KILNER

199 The Bright Key
Methuen, 1985. o.p. 0 4165 4500 9 (Pied Piper)

Judith's father turns to poaching when times get bad in 1830, but finds the law protects the animals not him so Judith is left alone to bring up the family after her father is outlawed. They are evicted in spite of paying the rent, and sent to the Poorhouse. Her father escapes to America, promising to send for them. A story of injustice, marred by the occasional false note.

IR 9+

Irina KORSCHUNOW

200 A Night in Distant Motion
Translated by Leigh Hartley
Hodder, 1984. o.p. 0 3403 6116 7 (Germany 1979)

Regine is a loyal Nazi until she meets Jan, a Polish POW working in her local shop. They fall in love but are caught together and Regine is imprisoned. Regine escapes in a raid and is taken in at a farm where she had worked the previous summer. This story of the last few months of the war is told in flashbacks, rather American and staccato in style, but moving nevertheless.

IR 12+

Elisabeth KYLE

201 The Key of the Castle
Illustrated by Joanna Troughton
Heinemann, 1976. o.p. 4349 4922 1 (Long Ago Children)

A brief and exciting retelling of the escape from Lochleven Castle of Mary, Queen of Scots, with the help of Willie Douglas. It varies in detail from other accounts, and is spoiled by truly awful illustrations.

IR 8+

Christa LAIRD

202 The Forgotten Son

Julia MacRae, 1990. 0 8620 3477 9

The author has taken the story of Heloise and Abelard further to construct in fiction the life of their baby, Peter. He is brought up by Heloise's sister Denise, but does meet his real parents. Twelfth-century France is beautifully described, but above all this is a story of the search for his parents by the son of their love.

IR 14+

203 Shadow of the Wall

Julia MacRae, 1989. 0 8620 3372 1
Walker, 1990. 0 7445 1759 1

The last few months of the orphanage run by Dr Janus Korczak in the Warsaw ghetto is seen through the eyes of Misha, who sees his mother fade before his eyes, his younger sister smuggled outside the ghetto for a non-Jewish family to bring up, and his beloved sister Rachel marched to the death camp at Treblinka with Dr Korczak and the rest of the orphans. A marvellous and inspiring story told with skill and emotion.

IR 10+

Rose Wilder LANE

204 **Let the Hurricane Roar**
Illustrated by Mary Thelander and Bob Geary
Puffin, 1982. o.p. 0 1403 1401 6 (USA 1933)

The daughter of Laura Ingalls Wilder published this novel before the Wilder books. Read after them it is disappointing because of the great similarity in episodes, but read alone it is a moving account of a young couple's fight to survive in the prairie.

IR 10+

Ann LAWRENCE

205 **Mr Robertson's Hundred Pounds**
With drawings by Elisabeth Trimby
Kestrel, 1976. o.p. 0 7226 5183 X

Simon is apprenticed to a Mr Robertson, from whom Matthew Butler steals one hundred pounds. Mr Robertson follows Butler across Europe to Spain, becoming involved in deception as England and Spain are at war. Simon discovers his vocation and a true friend. They recover part of the money and return to Elizabethan England full of information for Robert Cecil about the Spanish defences and shipbuilding. The deep characterization and a fine mature story make this a memorable experience.

IR 12+

Alec LEA

206 **To Sunset and Beyond**
Hamilton, 1970. o.p. 2410 1969 9

Peter helps by getting the cows in while the rest of the family rush to get the hay in before the storm. But the cows have strayed and he follows them on to the high moor at dusk. A poetic description of the harshness of farming life at the end of the last century, and of the cruelty of Dartmoor, yet a warming picture of a farming family and the day when a boy grew up.

IR 9+

Robert LEESON

207 Maroon Boy
Collins, 1974. o.p. 0 0067 2097 8 (Fontana)
Armada, 1982. 0 0067 2097 8

Matthew Morten sails as his master's quartermaster on a slaving run to Africa in the 1560s, but finds the cargo disgusts him. He frees the slaves and joins them (known as the Cimarroons) to wage war on the Spaniards. Eventually he returns home, but not to the hero's welcome he expects. This is a thought-provoking story with some depth.

IR 14+

208 Bess
Collins, 1975. o.p. 0 0018 4051

Bess is Matthew Morten's half-sister unaware she is. When she meets him, she has had an accident and lost her memory. After a failure to contract a marriage to the Cimarroon tribal chief's son, she returns to Plymouth and marries in order to have control of her money. This almost adult novel, a sequel to *Maroon Boy*, ranges far and wide in telling of a spirited girl in the early seventeenth century.

IR 14+

209 The White Horse
Collins, 1977. o.p. 0 0018 4925 5

The third story in the trilogy in which the half-caste son of Bess comes to England to avenge his father's death and his mother's treatment by her new husband, Ferrars. Morten becomes a bodyguard to Cromwell, while still seeking vengeance, and in the ends finds revenge is not what he thought. A sweeping novel of Cromwell's years in power, with the political scene as a backdrop.

IR 14+

Alison LEONARD

210 An Inch of Candle
Angus & Roberston, 1980. o.p. 0 2079 5936 6
Armada, 1982. 0 0067 2134 6 (Lions)

Dora, fifteen in 1916 and filled with patriotic fervour, is disgusted that her brother Richard is a conscientous objector. Through an encounter with the Reverend Bosanquet, her attitude changes as she reads some of his son's uncensored letters from the Front and the horror of the war is brought home to her. A sympathetic story of a girl growing up at a difficult time and overcoming tragedy in a brave and funny way. 'An inch of candle' is a quotation from a poem by Isaac Rosenberg.

IR 12+

Hilda LEWIS

211 The Gentle Falcon
Illustrated by Evelyn Gibbs
Oxford, 1952. 1927 7037 3

A rich story of Isabella Clinton and Isabel, child Queen of Richard II, brought from France to marry the king and thrust into the intrigue of court and the struggle for power. Old-fashioned now in that it deals with the lives of Kings and Queens, but painting a vivid picture of the period.

IR 10+

212 Here Comes Harry
Illustrated by William Stobbs
Oxford, 1960. o.p.

The boyhood of Henry VI is seen through the eyes of another fatherless boy, Harry Rushden, older than Henry but loyal to him. Harry becomes a spy for the Beauforts, ideally placed in his work as goldsmith's apprentice to do this. A shrewd study of the loneliness of a child who is a pawn in other men's pursuit of power.

IR 10+

Joan LINGARD

213 Tug of War
Hamilton, 1989. 0 2411 2816 1
Puffin, 1991. 0 1403 4323 7 (Plus)

Based on the family story of the author's husband, this tells of the Peterson family's flight from Latvia during the Second World War. Hugo is separated from the family including his twin, Astra, and is sheltered by a German family. After four years they are reunited and set out for a new life in Canada. A well-written book with some harrowing moments.

IR 12+

214 Between Two Worlds
Hamilton, 1991, 0 2411 1312 7

This sequel to *Tug of War*, continues the Peterson family's story as they arrive in Canada in 1948. Lukas, the father, has a heart attack and is unable to work, but Hugo and Astra find menial jobs, work hard, and get enough money to buy a plot of land for a house.

IR 12+

215 The File on Fraulein Berg
Julia MacRae. 1980. o.p. 0 8620 3000 5
Beaver, 1985. 0 0993 8290 3

Three Belfast schoolgirls convince themselves that the new teacher who has come to the school, and is German, is a spy. They follow her and keep a diary of her movements. Long after the war they discover she was a German-Jewish refugee. A very real picture of girls brought up in an atmosphere of war and hysteria, and an often amusing study of how people coped with the shortages imposed on them.

IR 10+

Penelope LIVELY

216 Boy Without a Name
Illustrated by Ann Dalton
Heinemann, 1975. o.p. 0434 9496 7 (Long Ago Children)

An orphan boy, without even a name, arrives in a small Cotswold village in the time of Charles I and by chance is apprenticed to a stone mason. He finds his future and a name as well. The small details of the life of a child without a welfare state to care for him, and the redoubtable character of the boy, make this a quite perfect book.

IR 7+

217 Fanny and the Battle of Potter's Piece
Illustrated by John Lawrence
Heinemann, 1980. o.p. 0 4349 4937 X (Long Ago Children)

A lively story of the Stanton children's battle with their new neighbours' children, over the waste ground where

From H. Burton, *Riders of the Storm*

they played. Full of details of the lives of middle-class children in Victorian England, and told with humour.

IR 8+

218 Fanny and the Monsters
Illustrated by John Lawrence
Heinemann, 1979. o.p. 4349 4935 3 (Long Ago Children)

Fanny meets a professor of palaeontology at the British Museum, and then encounters a fossil skeleton at a quarry. She is truly irrepressible in spite of having to behave as a Victorian middle-class child.

IR 8+

219 Fanny's Sister
Illustrated by John Lawrence
Heinemann, 1976. o.p. 4349 4924 8 (Long Ago Children)

Fanny, the eldest of the family, asks God for cherry tart for dessert and to take back her new sister. When the cherry tart appears, she decides to run away in case the other part comes true too! The vicar, to whom she runs, comes to the rescue. A glorious story, perfect to read aloud.

IR 8+

The three stories about Fanny (Nos 217–9) are published in one volume:

Heinemann, 1983. 0 4349 4888 8
Mammoth, 1991. 0 7497 9600 7
Puffin, 1982. 0 1403 1501 2

Rutgers van der LOEFF

220 Children on the Oregon Trail

Translated from the Dutch by Roy Edwards
Illustrated by Peggy Fortnum
Brockhampton, 1971. o.p. 3401 4942 6 (Netherlands 1954)
Puffin, 1970. 0 1403 0172 0

The innocuous beginning belies the stark horror of the death
of the parents of the seven Sager children on the westward
trail in 1844. John, the eldest, decides to go on as this was
his father's dream, but the journey becomes a nightmare. A
marvellous tale of endurance and courage, based on fact.

IR 10+

Lois LOWRY

221 Number the Stars

Collins, 1990. 0 0018 416 0
Armada, 1991. 0 0067 3677 7 (USA 1989)

Anne-Marie and her friend Ellen find living in occupied
Denmark difficult in 1943, but when the Jews start to be
rounded up Anne-Marie and her family help Ellen and her
family to escape. Aimed at a younger age group than most
books on this subject, it is a well-written story, not glossing
over the horror, or the courage needed to face it.

IR 8+

Elizabeth LUTZEIER

222 No Shelter

Blackie, 1984. o.p. 0 2169 1630 5
Canongate, 1986. 0 8624 1129 7 (Kelpie)
(Kathleen Fidler Award 1984)

Two German children aged eight and three, whose mother has been killed and whose father is away at the front, set off to find relations. They are taken in by some Germans who are anti-Hitler, and then when the Russians arrive set out for Stuttgart to find an uncle. An interesting picture of propaganda-fed children, and the chaos of war and its aftermath.

IR 9+

Geraldine McCAUGHREAN

223   A Little Lower Than the Angels
Oxford, 1987. 0 1927 6077 7
Puffin, 1989. 0 1403 2818 1

Gabriel runs away from his apprenticeship to a mason and literally falls into the Mystery plays. He looks like an angel so that is what he plays, and is used by the playmaster to deceive crowds into thinking that he can perform miracles. Gabriel comes to believe this himself, but then the mason catches up with him and he sees the truth. A frightening encounter with the Plague changes things but then Gabriel starts to act rather than be. An interesting (if at times complex) insight into the medieval Mystery plays.

IR 9+

Elsie McCUTCHEON

224   Rat War
Dent, 1985. 0 4600 6181 X

In post-Second World War Suffolk amid an epidemic of rats, Nicholas, deserted by his more gregarious sister, befriends a rat and feeds it secretly. But his world literally blows to pieces. Nicholas emerges from this experience a stronger, more confident person. A beautifully written book, very funny at times, about a boy conquering his fears. There are many details of post-war life, rationing and so on.

IR 9+

225 Summer of the Zeppelin
Dent, 1983. o.p. 0 4600 6133 X
Puffin, 1984. 0 1403 1661 2

Elivira lives with her stepmother and little brother in a small village, and meets a German POW in an old house she uses as a sanctuary. Her attempt to help Bill to escape fails, but there is a happy (if slightly pat) ending. A perceptive study of a girl coming to terms with her stepmother while her father is away at the Front, in a village taken over by war fever. A Zeppelin actually does appear.

IR 10+

Elisabeth MACE

226 Brother Enemy
Deutsch, 1979. o.p. 0 2339 7081 9

Andreas, half-Jewish is sent from Hamburg in the 1930s to live in England, leaving behind his mother and stepbrother. He is passed from person to person, unsettled and unwilling to come to terms with his half-Jewishness. Through Hope, a cockney evacuee, and Fred Aspinall the gravedigger, he is helped but returns to Hamburg to face reality. A complex and very gloomy book unrelieved by any warmth, and requiring maturity from the reader.

IR 12+

Jean MACGIBBON

227 A Special Providence: the Story of the Children in the Mayflower
Illustrated by William Stobbs
Hamilton, 1964. o.p.

The story of the events leading to the departure of the *Mayflower* and then of the voyage itself, told through the eyes of Giles Hopkinson. Based on fact and realistically told, it is an exciting account, and one of the few stories on the subject.

IR 9+

Eloise Jarvis McGRAW

228 Mara Daughter of the Nile
Puffin, 1985. o.p. 0 1403 1929 8 (USA 1953)

Mara becomes a double spy in a battle for the throne in Ancient Egypt. She falls in love with one of her masters but her double role is uncovered and she nearly loses all. A somewhat swashbuckling story with a difficult historical background which does give some details of life at the time. There is no glossary of terms and no map, both of which would have been very useful.

IR 12+

Patricia MACLACHLAN

229 Sarah, Plain and Tall
Julia MacRae, 1986. 0 8620 3247 4 (USA 1985)

In the nineteenth century Sarah arrives, in answer to an advertisement, to be a wife to Jacob and mother to Anna and Caleb. But she comes from the coast of Maine to the prairie and the children are afraid she will not stay after her month's trial. Beautiful, spare prose tells the story, but so much more is conveyed of the children's need for a mother and a happy father. A marvellous experience which should not be missed.

IR 8+

Michelle MAGORIAN

230 Back Home
Viking Kestrel, 1985. 0 6708 0670 6
Puffin, 1987. 0 1403 1907 7

Rusty returns to post-Second World War England after five years as an evacuee in a close family in America, to a quite different home with an appalling grandmother and a father who does not seem to want her. She is sent away to school but does not fit in there. A story which occasionally goes over the top, this does however point out the difficulties that could have been encountered.

IR 10+

231 Goodnight Mister Tom
Kestrel, 1981. o.p. 0 7226 5701 3
Puffin, 1983. 0 1403 1541 1 (Guardian Award 1982)

A small boy evacuated to the country from London, ends up with old Mister Tom. The boy's mother had beaten him regularly, but gradually Tom wins his trust and he settles down. There is an horrific episode when the boy returns to London. Basically an overlong, but absorbing study of relationships against the background of the Second World War.

IR 10+

Craig MAIR

232   The Lighthouse Boy
Illustrated by Ray Evans
Murray, 1981. o.p. 0 7195 5824 6

A detailed story of the construction of the Bell Rock lighthouse off the coast of Arbroath, designed and built by Robert Stevenson, grandfather of Robert Louis Stevenson. Based on fact, it tells the story of Jamie who ran away to support his family by working on the Rock.

IR 9+

Ruth MANNING-SANDERS

233   The Spaniards Are Coming
Illustrated by Jacqueline Rizin
Heinemann, 1968. o.p. 4349 4902 7 (Long Ago Children)

Two children, whose father has been taken for the Navy to fight the Armada, make their way across England to their uncle at Saltash. They meet with a pedlar and foil a robbery before they arrive safely. A jolly tale with some dialect, which would read aloud well.

IR 7+

Moira MILLER

234   Masque for a Queen
Methuen, 1987. o.p. 0 4169 7292 5 (Teens)

Another retelling of the imprisonment of Mary, Queen of Scots in Lochleven Castle and of Willie Douglas's part in her escape disguised as a washerwoman. Readable, but without the depth of the Mollie Hunter story.

IR 12+

E. MITCHELL

235 Light Horse to Damascus
Illustrated by Victor Ambrus
Hutchinson, 1971. o.p. 0 0910 6040

Told from the point of view of the horse, this is the story of Karloo and his rider Dick in the Middle East in 1914 and of the part the Australian Light Horse played in the war. Between the two is a strong bond and this carries them through the battles. A book for horse lovers but also of general interest because it covers a little-known part of the First World War.

IR 10+

Alison MORGAN

236 The Eyes of the Blind
Oxford, 1986. 0 1927 1542 9

Benjamin, the grandson of Isaiah, is in Jerusalem with his father when the Assyrians besiege the city. He is sent away to escape but stops to help a boy who turns out to be the son of the Assyrian general. Benjamin and Adad journey together and learn much about each other. A difficult book, not with immediate appeal, but dealing with an unusual topic.

IR 12+

Michael MORPURGO

237 Friend or Foe
Illustrated by Trevor Stubley
Methuen, 1984. o.p. 0 4164 6640 6

A seemingly straightforward story of two boys evacuated to Devon during the Second World War. David in particular hates the Germans who killed his father, but when a German saves him from drowning he finds his loyalties divided. Excellent characterization, particularly of Tucky, and good illustrations enhance a thoughtful story, marred only by a cover misleading as to age of intended readership.

IR 8+

238 Twist of Gold
Kaye & Ward, 1983. o.p. 0 7182 3971 7

Sean and Annie O'Brien cross from Ireland to America in 1847 and are befriended in Boston before travelling on to California to meet up with their father. Based on fact, this is a heartwarming, occasionally sentimental story.

IR 9+

239 Waiting for Anya
Heinemann, 1990. 0 6708 3735 0

Jo lives in Vichy France helping his mother with the sheep now that his father is a POW. A chance encounter leads him to help in the hiding of Jewish children waiting to escape over the mountain to Spain. Then the Germans come to the village and he learns that some of them can be human beings, but in an exciting ending two of the children are caught. A vivid and true picture of a small community drawn into the war.

IR 10+

240 War Horse
Kaye & Ward, 1982. 0 7182 3970 9
Magnet, 1983. 0 4162 9600 9

Joey, the horse, tells his own story: how he was befriended by Albert before the First World War and trained by him. Then bought by the Army he sees war and its suffering before being reunited with Albert. A warm, occasionally sentimental, and unusual view of the war.

IR 9+

Linda NEWBERY

241 Some Other War

Armada, 1990. 0 0069 3614 8 (Lions)

Twins Jack and Alice are both in service at the start of the First World War which changes both their lives. Alice finds emancipation as a nurse, and Jack discovers his courage in the trenches. Alice gradually realizes that a better life could exist for her and other women, and Jack contracts a hasty marriage. First part of a trilogy, this gets deeper as the reader becomes more involved.

IR 12+

From R. Welch, *Captain of Foot*

242 The Kind Ghosts

Armada, 1991. o.p. 0 0069 4117 6 (Lions)

This continues the story of *Some Other War* with Jack and Alice finding that the war has changed things. Jack's wife leaves him and Alice's engagement to Philip comes to an end. Very readable and full of detail.

IR 12+

243 The Wearing of the Green
Armada, 1992. 0 0067 4306 4 (Lions)

The third part of the trilogy, in which Patrick returns home from Gallipoli to convalesce in Ireland. He is Anglo-Irish and finds his loyalties divided when he is caught up in the 1916 Easter Rising in Dublin. An interesting and brave attempt to deal with the Irish Question, which a reader with no knowledge of the background might find difficult to follow.

IR 12+

Michael NOONAN

244 McKenzie's Boots
Orchard, 1989. 1 8521 3174 8 (Australia 1987)
Orchard, 1989. 1 8521 3145 4

At the age of fifteen Rod joins up to fight against the Japanese and has to have a pair of boots specially made for his large feet. The war in the jungle is made more personal when Rod and a Japanese soldier come face to face hunting the same butterfly. Rod dies a hero at seventeen and his boots are kept by his friend Nugget who tells the story. An unusual and thought-provoking book set outside Europe, which will remind readers of the other theatres of war.

IR 12+

Scott O'DELL

245 My Name is Not Angelica
Viking, 1991. 0 6708 3468 8

Raisha and the young chief she is to marry are sold as slaves and work on a Danish plantation on the island of St

John. The slaves revolt and there is a stand-off with an inevitable ending. A stark and moving story set in the eighteenth century, it adds to the books about slaves.

IR 12+

246 Streams to the River, River to the Sea
Viking, 1988. o.p. 0 6708 1904 2
Puffin, 1990. 0 1403 2466 6 (Plus)

An Indian girl is used to guide Lewis and Clark through the Rockies on their expedition from St Louis to the Pacific in 1801. The arduous journey is vividly described, and the girl's observation of the white settlers and her own people makes interesting reading.

IR 12+

Judith O'NEILL

247 Jess and the River Kids
Hamilton, 1984. 0 2411 1183 8

Tomboy Jess befriends two boys and an old lady who live in houseboats down on the river in a small Australian town during the Second World War. Lizzie tells Jess of her Northumbrian childhood, and Jess teaches the boys to paint. A fire changes all their lives. A sympathetic portrait of a friendship between young and old against a background of Australia at war.

IR 9+

248 So far from Skye
Hamilton, 1992. 0 2411 3213 4
Puffin, 1993. 0 7497 0392 X

Morag MacDonald and her family have to leave their croft in Skye after the failure of the potato crop in the 1850s and make the arduous journey to Australia for a better life. This journey is told in considerable and often harrowing detail, but the family find friends and work in Victoria. A deeply satisfying novel based on Judith O'Neill's own family history.

IR 12+

249 Stringybark Summer
Hamilton, 1985. o.p. 0 2411 1698 8
Mammoth, 1990. 0 7497 0392 X

Sophie is sent from the city in turn-of-the-century Australia to stay with her uncle, a country blacksmith, while her mother has a baby. She finds the transition difficult but learns to love the freedom and the life. A warm family story with a spirited heroine.

IR 9+

Jenny OVERTON

250 The Ship from Simnel Street
Faber, 1975. o.p. 0 5711 3649 4

Polly and Susannah, daughters of the baker in a small Sussex town in the middle of the eighteenth century, bake cakes for all the twelve hundred men of Polly's sweetheart's regiment. The details of this and the other domestic details, against the background of men leaving for the Peninsular War, make a delightful story.

IR 12+

Katherine PATERSON

251 Lyddie
Gollancz, 1991. 0 5750 5180 9

When the family have to split up after her father has left to look for work and her mother is unable to cope, Lyddie seeks work, first in a tavern and then in a textile factory. Her aim is to pay off the debts incurred and regain the family farm. Friendship with a radical jeopardizes all this, but gives her courage to find a new life and to go to college. Set in Lowell, Massachusetts in 1843, this is a low-key story with considerable impact.

IR 12+

See **Philippa PEARCE, no. 116**

K.M. PEYTON

252 **Flambards**
Illustrated by Victor Ambrus
Oxford, 1967. 0 1927 1278 0
Puffin, 1989. 0 1403 2620 0 (Plus)
Trilogy (Nos 252–4) won the Carnegie Medal in 1969

Orphaned Christina is sent to live with her Uncle Russell and his two sons, Will and Mark. It is a hunting household with the exception of Will who is absorbed by aeroplanes. Apart from Will and Dick, the stable boy, she finds it a hard, loveless existence. Set in the years leading up to the First World war.

IR 10+

253 **The Edge of the Cloud**
Illustrated by Victor Ambrus
Oxford, 1969. 0 1927 1298 5
Puffin, 1989. 0 1403 2621 9 (Plus)

The setting changes in the second part of the trilogy, when Will runs away to be with his beloved aeroplanes and Christina joins him. The early flying is very dangerous and Christina fears for his safety. A marvellous evocation of the pioneering days of flight, and a deeper story than the first book.

IR 12+

254 Flambards in Summer

Illustrated by Victor Ambrus
Oxford, 1969. 0 1927 1312 4
Puffin, 1977. 0 1403 0938 1

After Will is killed in the war, Christina returns to Flambards, pregnant and hoping to make something of the house now that she has control of her father's money. Mark is missing, but Dick returns from the war and their relationship progresses, although set back by Mark's return.

IR 12+

255 Flambards Divided

Oxford, 1981. 0 1927 1452 X
Puffin, 1988. 0 1403 2515 8 (Plus)

In this addition to the trilogy, Christina marries Dick, despite misgivings, but Mark's return threatens her marriage and in the end the differences between her and Dick prove irreconcileable. A good picture of a marriage where love is not enough to overcome the differences. A mature book and the right ending to the series.

IR 14+

256 The Maplin Bird

Illustrated by Victor Ambrus
Oxford, 1964. o.p. 0 1927 1238 1

Emily and Toby sail away from their cruel relations in their late father's fishing smack. Emily finds work on the Essex coast as a housemaid, discovering that the son of the house is an accomplished smuggler. She falls under his spell and Toby tries to help him by sailing the *Maplin Bird* to freedom. The poverty and class distinctions of nineteenth-century England are well drawn, as is the handsome Adam's amorality. Victor Ambrus's marvellous drawings enhance the book enormously.

IR 12+

257 The Right-Hand Man

Illustrated by Victor Ambrus
Oxford, 1977. o.p. 0 1927 1391 4

Ned goes to work as a coachman for Ironminster, a sick man, and helps him to win a wager, but the cost is high and Ned ends up in Newgate Gaol, to be freed only by a compromise and a price. A fine evocation of the contrast between the grace and sordidness of life in 1818–19; there is an interesting picture of the gaol, and loyalty to one's friends and pride in work is manifest.

IR 12+

258 Thunder in the Sky

Illustrated by Victor Ambrus
Oxford, 1966. o.p.
Red Fox, 1990. 0 0997 5150 X

Sam and Gil work on sailing barges along the coast, Manny their elder brother has enlisted and is in the trenches during the First World War. Sam discovers that Gil is mixed up in something and, when he finds out what, makes an epic journey to see Manny to get advice. There is a satisfying denouement to this stark tale of life on the barges plying across the Channel with their dangerous cargo of coal and ammunition. A deep, morally satisfying book which does not spare the reader.

IR 12+

259 Windfall

Illustrated by Victor Ambrus
Oxford, 1962. o.p.

After the death of his father, Matt takes on his ageing fishing smack and the support of the family and tries to earn enough money for a new smack. An encounter with Francis

Shelley, a rich man's son, seems to be the turning point although the sinister Beckett is in the background waiting his chance. A sea story, pure and simple with the hard work and poverty involved beautifully depicted, and well illustrated. Set on the Essex coast in the late nineteenth century.

IR 12+

B. L. PICARD

260 Lost John
Illustrated by Charles Keeping
Oxford, 1962. o.p.

A powerful story of a boy driven to seek revenge for his father's death at the hands of Sir Raoul. He is captured by the outlaws led by Sir Ralf, only to find that he is Raoul. A vivid picture of the lawlessness of life under King John, in the absence of Richard I. Strong illustrations by Charles Keeping straddle the pages and enforce the mood of the story.

IR 10+

261 One is One
Illustrated by Victor Ambrus
Oxford, 1965. o.p.

The son of a thirteenth-century knight, Stephen is sent to a monastery. Here he finds his place as his talent for drawing develops, but his past failures are revived by a visit from his brother so he runs away, determined to become a knight and prove himself. He achieves this but returns to the monastery to illustrate the Gospels. A tremendous amount of historical detail fills the book and illuminates the period well, helped considerably by Victor Ambrus's lovely drawings.

IR 12+

262 Ransom for a Knight
Illustrated by C. Walter Hodges
Oxford, 1956. o.p.

Lady Alys, alone but for Hugh, the ploughman's son, carries the ransom for her father and brother from Sussex to Scotland after the Battle of Bannockburn, a journey that takes them twenty months. A detailed picture of life in medieval England emerges, and the class system is clearly drawn in the relationship between the two.

IR 10+

Stephanie PLOWMAN

263 Three Lives for the Czar
Bodley, 1969. o.p. 3700 1204 6 (New Adults)

The reign of Czar Nicholas II up to the outbreak of the First World War is seen through the eyes of Andrei Hamilton, a French-Russian solder, whose mother is a lady-in-waiting to the Czarina. The story moves all across Europe and does require some knowledge of European politics at the time. It shows clearly the inevitability of the fall of the Czar.

IR 14+

264 My Kingdom for a Grave
Bodley, 1970. o.p. 0 3700 1217 8

In the sequel to *Three Lives for the Czar*, Andrei is still faithful to Nicholas and follows him through the revolution to his fate at Ektarinburg. Almost adult in content, this is a detailed and complex story but well worth reading.

IR 14+

265 To Spare the Conquered
Methuen, 1960. o.p.

From R. Sutcliff, *Knight's Fee*

Quintus Valerius Martius comes to Britain with the Roman Legions and becomes Suetonius' Chief of Staff. He tells of the rising of the Iceni under Boadicea and the bloody battle that ensues. It is an interesting and sympathetic study of the events, which does require some understanding of the background from the reader.

IR 12+

Elsa POSELL

266 Homecoming
Heinemann, 1984. o.p. 4349 5660 0
Mammoth, 1989. 0 7497 0050 5

An autobiogaphical novel of the author's experiences during the Russian revolution. Her family were Jews and suffered badly. After her father fled for his life, his wife and six children had to fend for themselves. Hunger was the greatest problem and the mother dies of malnutrition. Eventually the family escape to Poland and thence to America to join their father. A harrowing and sad picture with the ring of truth.

IR 12+

Rhoda POWER

267 Redcap Runs Away
Illustrated by C. Walter Hodges
Cape, 1952. o.p. 0 2240 0503 0

Redcap runs away to search for his great uncle who ran away in his turn to be a minstrel. He meets up with two minstrels, Fulk Nial and Jack Piper and travels with them, learning and searching. The story is interspersed with old tales and details of medieval life and could well be acted out or read aloud. Has not really dated as it is so lively.

IR 9+

Susan PRICE

268 Christopher Uptake
Faber, 1981. 0 571 1160

Christopher rebels against his university's strict regime and is drawn to the world of the theatre. He starts to write plays and leaves the university to pursue this career, and half knowingly he gives information about the whereabouts of Catholics and is caught in a trap. A deep and dark study of a boy trapped into spying for Elizabeth I's men who are out to catch Catholics. A difficult and demanding book about bigotry at its worst.

IR 14+

269 Twopence a Tub
Faber, 1975. o.p. 0 571 10624 2
Faber, 1991. 0 5711 6125 1

A stark picture of a mining community near Dudley in the 1850s, and of a strike broken by grinding poverty and hardship, is seen through the eyes of Jek, eldest of a mining family. A somewhat one-sided portrayal.

IR 12+

Alison PRINCE

270 How's Business
Marilyn Malin/Deutsch, 1987. o.p. 0 23398 0385
Pan, 1989. 0 3303 0485 2 (Piper)

How goes to stay with his aunt and uncle in Lincolnshire because of the bombing. He finds it hard to settle and be accepted but takes the dare offered by the boys and succeeds. He makes friends with a refugee girl, and travels to London to see if his Mum is all right when he does not hear from her. All this is gently told, very believably painting a picture of the strain that war put on a small boy. It was written by a class of children according to the author's foreword. A real gem.

IR 9+

Philip PULLMAN

271 The Ruby in the Smoke
Oxford, 1985. 0 1927 1543 7
Puffin, 1987. 0 1403 2209 4

Orphaned Sally becomes involved in a complex plot involving opium smuggling in the Far East and the quest for a ruby. It is a rattling good yarn with some good feel for the Victorian setting.

IR 12+

272 The Shadow in the Plate
Oxford, 1986. 0 1927 1548 8
Puffin, 1988. 0 1403 2648 0 (Title: *The Shadow in the North*)

This sequel to *The Ruby in the Smoke* follows Sally's exploits as a financial adviser which lead her into more adventures with Fred, now a detective as well as a photographer. Jam-packed with twists and turns, and somewhat implausible at times, but with some good insights into life at the time, especially the plight of women.

IR 14+

273 The Tiger in the Well

Viking, 1991. 0 6708 3279 0
Puffin, 1992. 0 1403 4484 5 (Plus)

Sally now has Harriet, her two-year-old illegitimate daughter by the deceased Fred, but in a marvellously twisted plot
Harriet is taken from her. Sally meets Daniel Goldberg, a
Jewish activist, and sees deprivation and poverty at first
hand, thus finding her vocation, as well as love. This has
more social awareness than the other stories, and takes a
sharp look at anti-Semitism.

IR 14+

David REES

274 The Exeter Blitz

Hamilton, 1978. o.p. 0 241 89759 9
Heinemann, 1981. 0 435 12258 4 (Windmill)
(Carnegie Medal 1978)

Colin Lockwood sees the bombing of Exeter on the night of
3 and 4 May, 1942 from the Cathedral tower. It is an exciting sight to see but then he begins to be anxious about his
family. Eventually he finds them but it is a worrying time.
A quiet story which allows the full horror of the night to
slowly impinge upon the reader.

IR 10+

275 The Green Bough of Liberty

Dobson, 1979. 0 2347 2187 1

The Byrne family, Farrett, Billy and Ned, are caught up in
the United Irish movements and they fight in the rebellion of 1798 against the British rule. Billy is hanged, although protesting his innocence; Ned struggles with his
conscience after killing a soldier, and is captured but rescued. It is a rather one-sided account of events as, with

the odd exception, all British soldiers are portrayed as sadistic thugs.

IR 12+

276 Landslip
Illustrated by Gavin Rowe
Hamilton, 1977. o.p. 0 2418 9539 1

There is drama in a Norfolk village in the late nineteenth century when a landslip makes the Powleys homeless. George, Josie and Sarah Collins explore the landslip and Josie witnesses another and is marooned, but it is Sarah who is hurt going for help. A small incident rounded out with domestic detail to give a picture of rural life. A large format book with good illustrations.

IR 8+

Johanna REISS

277 The Upstairs Room
Oxford, 1973. o.p. 0 1927 1354 X (USA 1972)
Longman, 1991. 0 5820 5804 X (Sky)

A Jewish mother writes for her daughters a barely fictional-ised account of how she and her older sister were hidden for two years by a Dutch family during the Second World War. The kindness and the deprivation are described, and the feeling of being shut in one room for two years is quite overwhelming.

IR 10+

Elizabeth RENIER

278 The Mail-Coach Driver
Illustrated by Eric Stemp
Hamilton, 1985. o.p. 0 2411 1654 6 (Antelope)

Based on a real event in 1816, this tells of a boy sent to train as a gardener but who wants to be a Royal Mail coach driver and who, by dint of an encounter with an escaped lioness, moves a little nearer to his dream.

IR 7+

279 The Night of the Storm
Illustrated by Trevor Stubley
Hamilton, 1986. o.p. 0 2411 1912 X (Antelope)

May Bratton befriends the son of the local squire who then determines to tell his father of the danger that the dredging in Start Bay is doing by eroding the sea defences. After a big storm his father comes, and promises to stop dredging and pay all the damage. Based on a true story of dredging between 1897–1902, when a new sea wall had to be built but which did not prevent the village of Hallsands being destroyed in a storm in 1917. The ending has been changed.

IR 7+

Hans Peter RICHTER

280 Friedrich
Translated from the German by Edite Kroll
Kestrel, 1971. o.p. 0 7226 5285 2
Puffin, 1987. 0 1403 2205 1 (Germany 1961)

A chilling episodic story charts the progress of anti-Jewish feeling in Hitler's Germany, through the eyes of a German boy who lives in a block of flats, one of which is inhabited by a Jewish family. From 1925 to 1942 the telling little episodes mount up, unrelieved by any warmth. A remarkable experience.

IR 12+

281 I Was There
Translated from the German by Edite Kroll
Kestrel, 1973. o.p. 0 7226 6434 6
Puffin, 1987. 0 1403 2206 X (Germany 1962)

Second in the trilogy, with Hans, the narrator of *Friedrich*, telling his story through his time in the Hitler Youth to his enlistment in the army following his friend Heinz. Still told in the same episodic and effective style, this is a chilling experience.

IR 12+

282 The Time of the Young Soldiers
Translated by Anthea Bell
Kestrel, 1976. o.p. 0 7226 5122 8 (Germany 1967)

The third in the trilogy, in which Hans enlists, is wounded, loses an arm and becomes an officer. Still told in the same episodic style although not as frightening as the other two books, being more about soldiering than the persecution of the Jews.

IR 12+

Veronica ROBINSON

283 The Captive Isle
Illustrated by Geraldine Spence
Dent, 1960. o.p.

Mary lives on Jersey during the years of German occupation in the Second World War. The severity of life and the hardships are seen, with the children's acts of defiance and Mary's father's friendship with an old German friend giving an interesting view of life in the only part of England to be occupied.

IR 9+

Bill ROSEN

284 Andi's War
Faber, 1988. 0 5711 5144 2
Faber, 1989. 0 5711 5341 0

Andi and her brother Paul get caught up in the civil war in Greece after the Second World War. They live with their grandmother as their parents are fighting in the hills. They find some guns in a cave, but what begins as a game goes horribly wrong.

IR 10+

Fay SAMPSON

285 A Free Man on Sunday
Gollancz, 1987. 0 5750 4114 5
Lions, 1990. 0 0067 3501 0

Based on the true episode of the Mass Trespass on Kinder Scout in the Peak District in 1932, when a group of walkers exercised their right to walk freely, this tells of a girl whose father takes part in the walk.

IR 10+

286 Jenny and the Wreckers
Illustrated by Vanessa Julian-Ottie
Hamilton, 1984. o.p. 0 2411 1368 7 (Antelope)

Eight-year-old Jenny is left alone in the lighthouse while her widowed father goes shopping. He does not return at dusk to light the big oil light having been waylaid by wreckers, so Jenny summons up her courage and lights it. A moving account of a child's courage, fortified literally by the family Bible, and based on fact.

IR 7+

Ruth SAWYER

287 Roller Skates
Illustrated by Shirley Hughes
Bodley, 1964. o.p. 3700 0984 3 (USA 1936)

When Lucinda's parents go to Italy she stays in turn-of-the-century New York with the Misses Peter and finds a freedom not known before. On her roller skates she makes friends with everyone and although she encounters tragedy she overcomes this too before she has to return to her strait jacketed life as a late child of her parents. A book to put alongside *Anne of Green Gables* and *Little Women*, with its very American heroine.

IR 9+

288 Lucinda's Year of Jubilo
Illustrated by Shirley Hughes.
Bodley, 1965. o.p. (USA 1940)

Lucinda's father has died and the family, very poor and shattered at their loss, go to live at their summer cottage in Maine. They all work together, although Lucinda has trouble with her brother Carter. She fights her mother's pneumonia, gets her brother Duncan wed and gets hurt over her first love. Set in a Maine winter, this is a deep sequel to *Roller Skates*, with a heroine to admire.

IR 10+

Ann SCHLEE

289 Ask Me No Questions
Macmillan, 1976. o.p. 3331 9907 3

Laura finds out that next door to her aunt's house children are living in the most appalling conditions. Laura steals to feed three of these children and matters are brought to a head by her discovery of a dead girl in the barn, after which a cholera epidemic is uncovered. The strictness of Victorian society and the conditions of poverty in which

From R. Sutcliff, *Warrior Scarlet*

some people lived are well described, and stay in the mind for a long time. Based on fact.

IR 12+

290 The Consul's Daughter
Macmillan, 1972. o.p. 3331 3516 4

Based on fact, with a little embroidery, this is the story of the escape of the Consul's wife, daughter and baby son from Algiers after the confrontation between the Dey and Lord Exmouth in 1816. The somewhat detached style lends weight to the narrative and makes the bombardment of Algiers by the British fleet, which Anna and her step-mother witness, all the more horrific.

IR 12+

Jenny SEED

291 Canvas City
Illustrated by Lynette Hemmant
Hamilton, 1968. o.p. 2410 1556 1 (Reindeer)

Maggie, her parents and brother trek to find diamonds so that they can buy a sugar farm. But the diamond fever gets them and a big find just means a bigger mining claim can be bought. An exciting story about a little-known part of South African history.

IR 9+

292 The Red Dust Soldiers
Pictures by Andrew Sier
Heinemann, 1972. o.p. 4349 4906 X (Long Ago Children)

A boy goes from the camp of women and children to see his father in the besieged town of Ladysmith and witnesses its relief. An encounter with the Boers shows him that not all the enemy are bad. An interesting and well-written little story.

IR 8+

293 Strangers in the Land
Hamilton, 1976. o.p. 2418 9400 X

Mr Thompson, an Englishman, is totally unprepared for the life of a settler in South Africa. What sustains him is his faith in God, but his son Matthew finds this irksome and so he runs off with his friend Jeremiah. They are party to an horrifying elephant hunt and return home chastened. A good and exciting story with some depth.

IR 9+

Ian SERRAILLIER

294 The Silver Sword
Cape, 1956. 0 2246 0677 8
Puffin, 1970. 0 1403 0146 1

Ruth, Edek, and Bronia, joined by Jan, travel across post-war Europe from Poland through Germany to Switzerland, to find their parents. A marvellous tale of courage and endurance which has not dated at all, and which has become a classic. Based on a true story.

IR 9+

Margaretta SHEMIN

295 The Little Riders
Illustrated by Peter Spier
Julia MacRae, 1988. 0 8620 3400 0
Walker, 1990. 0 7445 1751 6

Johanna, staying with her grandparents, is caught in their home town in Holland when the Second World War begins. She helps to hide the little riders from the church tower, which the Germans want to melt down, and is aided in this by their German lodger. A deceptively slight tale with great charm.

IR 8+

Vian SMITH

296 Moon in the River
Illustrated by Anthony Colbert
Longmans, 1969. o.p. 5 8201 5307 7

Kurt, Onah and their father survive a massacre of their village on Dartmoor and flee. They make a hut from stones, and start life anew, making weapons. Kurt, the inventor, tries his hand at a kiln before being attacked by another tribe. An interesting reconstruction of the life of early man based on the hut circles on the moor.

IR 10+

Barbara SMUCKER

297 Underground to Canada
Penguin, 1978. 0 1403 1122 X (Canada 1977)

Liza and Julilly escape with two men from a Mississippi slave plantation. The men are captured but the girls stay free and journey on. Their travel north on the underground railway brings them into contact with real characters from the period. This fine story does gloss over the hardships somewhat, but the plight of the girls and their dignity in facing it are well told.

IR 9+

Barbara SOFTLY

298 Place Mill
Illustrated by Shirley Hughes
Macmillan, 1962. o.p.

Kate has not seen her brother since they witnessed the execution of their Royalist father for treason. She foils a plot to kill the King and finds this reunites her with Nicholas, and they start a new life together. The complexities of family relationships, and people's behaviour in times of stress are well pictured and make this a credible and exciting story. Set during the Civil War.

IR 10+

299 A Stone in a Pool
Illustrated by Shirley Hughes
Macmillan, 1964. o.p.

Stephen, a schoolboy at Newport Grammar school, becomes involved in plots to help the imprisoned Charles I escape. While working in disguise at Carisbrooke Castle he meets Henrietta, daughter of the Rector of Bonchurch, whom some think to be a witch. Some knowledge of the background of the Civil War is necessary to understand this story, which draws a good picture of fear and the insularity of village life.

IR 10+

Elizabeth George SPEARE

300 The Bronze Bow
Gollancz, 1962. o.p.
Puffin, 1970. 0 1403 0459 2
(USA 1960, Newbery Medal 1961)

Daniel has gone to a guerilla band in the mountains after the death of his father at the hands of the Romans. But he returns to the village to look after his withdrawn sister, and slowly comes to terms with his own hate and bitterness after listening to Jesus. A magnificent recreation of Israel at the time of Jesus which makes the reader feel he is there.

IR 10+

301 Calico Captive
Illustrated by W.T. Mars
Gollancz, 1970. o.p. 5750 0658 7 (USA 1957)

A reconstruction of events recorded in a diary, published in 1807, telling the courageous story of Miriam and Susannah Willard, captured together with James (Susannah's husband) and three children from a New England settlement in 1754. They are taken and sold to the French in Montreal where they have to wait for James's return with a ransom from the English settlers. A remarkable and absorbing story.

IR 12+

302 The Witch of Blackbird Pond
Gollancz, 1960. o.p. 5750 0225 5
Puffin, 1990. 0 1403 0327 8
(USA 1958, Newbery Medal 1959)

Kit Tyler arrives from Barbados with trunks full of lovely clothes to join her aunt's household with its strict Puritan religious principles in the New England of 1687. She befriends a Quaker lady deemed to be a witch, and stands trial herself before being saved by a sailor she met on the voyage. An enthralling story with much to say of the bigotry of strict religious sects, and also of a rule from England that was less than just.

IR 12+

Eleanor SPENCE

303 Lillipilly Hill
Illustrated by Susan Einzig
Oxford, 1960. o.p.

The Wilmot family arrive in Australia from England to settle on an uncle's estate but, except for Harriet and her
father, they want to return. Harriet decides on a course of
action and they stay. She is a determined and spirited young
lady and her relationships with other people, especially her
brother Aidan, are well drawn.

IR 9+

304 The Switherby Pilgrims
Illustrated by Corinna Gray
Oxford, 1967. o.p.

Miss Arabella Braithwaite takes ten orphans from England
in the 1820s, to New South Wales to find a better life. The
hardships they endured and the individual characters of
the children, especially Cassie and Francis, are well drawn.
There is much humour in this book, and the experiences
are interesting to compare with those of American settlers.

IR 9+

305 Jamberoo Road
Illustrated by Doreen Roberts
Oxford, 1969.

This sequel to *The Switherby Pilgrims* follows Cassie's
progress as a companion/governess to Gillis Marlow at
Falls Farm, Jamberoo Road. Cassie has to come to terms
with her feelings for Eban, and there are glimpses of
Missabella and the other orphans. Luke turns unwillingly
to crime, but all ends well. A deep, satisfying story with
much sense of place and time.

IR 10+

Alan SPOONER

306 Rainbow Cake
Illustrated by David Parkins
Kestrel, 1981. o.p. 0 7226 5675 0

Brian, who has lost his twin brother and then his closest
friend in the bombing, is sent to Aunt Julia's in the country
to recuperate. Here he finds Pip, the foster daughter, and
has to overcome his squeamishness about the farm, (and
the outside toilet!). He and Pip find a German airman hiding and in rescuing him Brian comes to terms with his pain.
A well-written and funny story, with deep characterization.

IR 9+

Noel STREATFEILD

307 Thursday's Child
Illustrated by Peggy Fortnum
Collins, 1970. o.p. 0 0018 4809 7

Irrepressible Margaret goes to an appalling orphanage and
is befriended by Lavinia, Peter and Horatia. After many
adventures she finds her place and the others find a grandfather. The plot covers life in a great house, an orphanage,
on a canal barge and in a travelling theatre in the late
nineteenth century. A good and enjoyable read.

IR 9+

308 Far to Go
Illustrated by Charles Mozley
Collins, 1976. o.p. 0 0018 4246 3

In the sequel to *Thursday's Child*, Margaret is a great success
as Little Lord Fauntleroy and answers an advertisement for
a young girl to act with Sir John Teason's company. A friendship with his daughter, a reunion with Lavinia and a kid-

nap by Matron make this a racy story in which the plight of children in late Victorian England is made clear.

IR 9+

Yuri SUHL

309 Uncle Misha's Partisans
Hamilton, 1975. o.p. 2418 9157 4 (USA 1973)
Shapolsky Books, 1988. 0 9335 0323 7

Inspired by an episode in the Ukraine during the Second World War, this is a moving story of a young Jewish boy who joins Uncle Misha's partisans in the forests. With his violin he takes part in some of the raids, culminating in the blowing up of the German officers' house on a Saturday night. Harrowing and sad at times.

IR 10+

Rosemary SUTCLIFF

310 The Armourer's House
Illustrated by C. Walter Hodges
Oxford, 1951. o.p.

Tamsyn goes to live in London with her aunt and Uncle Gideon, an armourer. During her first year she makes friends with Piers and finds they share a desire to go to sea. A warm, slightly sentimental story of a Tudor childhood.

IR 8+

311 Blood Feud
Oxford, 1976. o.p.
Puffin, 1978. 0 1403 1085 1

Jestyn is taken by the Vikings and sold as a thrall to Thormod, to whom he later becomes a blood-brother. Their

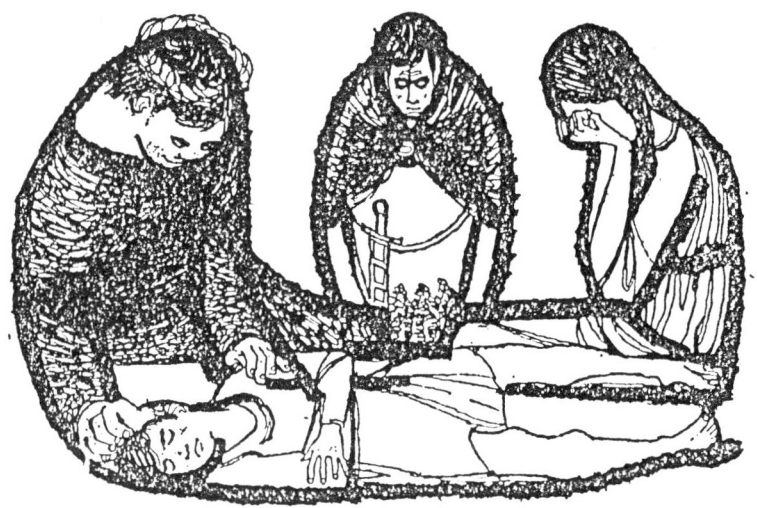

From R. Sutcliff, *The Lantern Bearers*

search for the two men who killed Thormod's father takes them to Kiev and then to Miklagard, where they become members of the Varogian Guard. After Thormod's death, Jestyn is invalided out and works as a healer. A vivid picture of the brotherhood of the Vikings, of Constantinople, and of a man finding his peace.

IR 12+

312 Bonnie Dundee

Bodley, 1983. o.p. 0 3703 0963 4
Puffin, 1985. 0 1403 1721 X

Hugh Herriot first sees John Graham of Claverhouse in action against the Covenanters, and finds himself following him when he tries to raise the Highlands for deposed James II. He sees him die at the battle of Killiecrankie in 1689 and, still loyal, follows the cause until wounded. As a painter in Rotterdam he looks back at his life. The skilful piecing of the complicated political background, the feeling of place which pervades the story, and the excellent characterization make this a memorable experience. A map and a glossary of Scottish terms would have been useful.

IR 12+

313 Brother Dusty-Feet
Illustrated by C. Walter Hodges
Oxford, 1952. o.p.

When Hugh's aunt threatens his dog he leaves home and takes the road to Oxford. He meets a band of travelling players and joins them to play the girls' parts. A tale of the Elizabethan theatre in which we see the first of Rosemary Sutcliff's portrayals of friendship between young men.

IR 10+

314 The Capricorn Bracelet
Illustrated by Charles Keeping
Oxford, 1973. o.p. 0 1927 1350 7
Red Fox, 1990. 0 0997 7620 0

Six stories of Roman Britain are linked by the silver Distinguished Conduct bracelet, handed down through generations of men from AD 61 to AD 383. All are told in beautiful prose and tell of man's honour and integrity as well as of his battles.

IR 10+

315 The Changeling
Illustrated by Victor Ambrus
Hamilton, 1974. o.p. 0 2418 9019 5 (Antelope)

Tethra is found as a baby in place of the chief's son taken by the Dark People. He faces a crisis and leaves the tribe, returning by chance to his own people, but finds his rearing and love of his foster father too strong to resist when the man is hurt. Best read aloud to enable the full power of the story to be felt.

IR 8+

316 The Chief's Daughter
Illustrated by Victor Ambrus
Hamilton, 1978. o.p. 0 3302 5444 4 (Antelope)
(First published in *The Eleanor Farjeon Book*, 1966)

A chief's daughter risks her life to save the life of the Irish boy, when the Wise Man sentences him to death because the water in the well has dried up. Told in a rich prose which would make it read aloud well, but might put off a younger reader.

IR 9+

317 A Circlet of Oak Leaves
Illustrated by Victor Ambrus
Hamilton, 1968. o.p.

Aracos, the ex-auxiliary now a horse-breeder, is a hero to the auxiliaries in the Rose and Wineskin because he won the Corona Civica, the circlet of oak leaves. But there is a mystery behind this, revealed to the reader alone. A marvellous story, not really suitable for the age group for whom this series is intended, but which would read aloud superbly to any age group.

IR 9+

318 Dawn Wind
Oxford, 1961. o.p.
Puffin, 1982. 0 1403 1223 4

At fourteen Owain finds himself alone after the Battle of Aquae Sulis. He and Dog befriend Regina and together they travel to find a boat to take them to Gaul. Regina is ill and to help her Owain becomes a thrall to Beornwulf on his farm on the south coast of Britain. He wins his freedom but relinquishes it to give him the chance to search for Regina. Finally he sees the dawn wind of a new Britain stirring with Augustine's arrival. A deep and complex novel told in beautiful language, full of the sight and sound of the countryside, and of the time.

IR 12+

319 The Eagle of the Ninth

Illustrated by C. Walter Hodges
Oxford, 1954. 0 1927 1037 0
Puffin, 1977. 0 1403 0890 3

Marcus is invalided out of the Roman army in Britain and decides to track down the lost eagle of the Ninth Legion with which his father served, and which marched away into the mists of northern Britain. Together with his freed slave, Esca, he searches north of the Wall for the eagle, symbol of the honour of the legion. Based on two events reconstructed into a linked whole, this is a tremendous evocation of early Britain, the tribes, and the Romans who ruled it. The first of three linked stories.

IR 12+

320 The Silver Branch

Illustrated by Charles Keeping
Oxford, 1957. o.p.
Puffin, 1980. 0 1403 1221 8

Flavius (a descendant of Marcus in *The Eagle of the Ninth*) and his surgeon cousin Justin, become involved in intelligence gathering in Britain as preparation for the day when Constantine comes to take the province back for Rome. A more political book than the above and peopled by historical characters, but it is Justin's story. Real-life heroes like Carausius and villains like Allectus march through the story, darkly illustrated by Charles Keeping. The second story in the sequence.

IR 12+

321 The Lantern Bearers

Illustrated by Charles Keeping
Oxford, 1959. o.p.
Puffin, 1991. 0 1403 1222 6
(Carnegie Medal 1959)

Aquila, a British officer in the Roman army, decides to stay when the Romans leave Britain. He returns to his home, only to see his father killed and his sister taken off by the Saxons, and he himself becomes a thrall to the old chieftain, Bruni in Jutland. But he returns to Britain with a band of settlers, escapes and joins Ambrosius's band, a bitter man nursing his hurt even into his marriage, until finally he is healed. A deep, complex portrait of a man finding himself, having to come to terms with his grief and pain, and an evocation of the early British race. The trilogy grows in depth and is a deeply satisfying experience, which many an adult would relish.

IR 12+

These three stories (Nos 319–21) are published together as
The Three Legions
Oxford, 1980. 0 1927 1450 3
Puffin, 1991. 0 1403 1222 6

322 Eagle's Eggs

Illustrated by Victor Ambrus
Hamilton, 1981. o.p. 0 2411 0620 6 (Antelope)

A brief story of Roman army life, told with humour, in which an eagle standard lays an egg, there is a meeting with a girl and some battles. There is no concession to the young reader in the language used and it would be more accessible if read aloud.

IR 9+

323 Frontier Wolf

Oxford, 1980. o.p. 0 1927 1448 1
Puffin, 1984. 0 1403 1472 5

A story of a Roman centurion sent to the northern frontier of Britain in disgrace to take command of the Third Ordo of Frontier Wolves. The smoke of the cooking fire, the sight of the bleak northern countryside, and the fear and feel of battle all assume reality as the reader is almost literally transported to another time.

IR 12+

From R. Sutcliff, *Simon*

324 Knight's Fee

Illustrated by Charles Keeping
Oxford, 1960. o.p.
Red Fox, 1990. 0 0997 7630 8

Randal, an orphan boy, finds his place as a foster-brother to Bevis, grandson of a knight, in a small manor in Sussex in Norman England. Randal and Bevis become close friends and share everything, except Bevis' vigil to become a knight. The Sussex downs, a favourite setting of Rosemary Sutcliff, feature greatly in this magnificent story.

IR 10+

325 The Mark of the Horse Lord

Oxford, 1965. o.p.
Puffin, 1983. 0 1403 1473 3

Phaedrus, a gladiator, takes the place of Midir, the Horse Lord of the Dalriads, to win the tribe back its lands from Liadhan the she-wolf, and finds he is worthy of the kingship. After a year-long battle it ends heroically with his death and Liadhan's at the Roman fort. Full of the sights and sounds of the hills and glens, and the beliefs of the early tribes of Britain.

IR 12+

326 Outcast

Illustrated by Richard Kennedy
Oxford, 1955. o.p.
Oxford, 1980. 0 1927 7106 X

Beric is found and taken in by the tribe, but then blamed for the bad harvest some years later and cast out. He is tricked into slavery, wrongly accused and then becomes a galley slave. He escapes, having been taken for dead, and finds a haven at last. A sad story redeemed by the happy ending; told with strength in rich prose.

IR 10+

327 The Queen Elizabeth Story
Illustrated by C. Walter Hodges
Oxford, 1950. o.p.

Perdita lives in the West Country and her dearest wish is to
see Elizabeth I. Details of her warm family life, her vivid
imagination and how her dream nearly does not come true
are described in a very rich prose, full of colour and love.

IR 8+

328 The Shield Ring
Illustrated by C. Walter Hodges
Oxford, 1956. o.p.

Saxon Frytha, a survivor of a Norman massacre, is taken by
the shepherd Grim to the settlement in the Lake District
ruled by Jarl Buthar. Here she becomes Bjorn's friend and
sees him through his own personal battle as well as the
final one. A moving story full of the skies and countryside
of the Lake District. Based on stories of the last battle between the Viking settlers in the Lake District, and the
Normans.

IR 10+

329 Shifting Sands
Illustrated by Laszlo Acs
Hamilton, 1977. o.p. 0 2418 9549 9 (Antelope)

Blue Feather catches the eye of Long Axe, the Chief of the
village, but when Singing Dog challenges the Chief's au-
thority she begins to have doubts about the marriage. The
Chief ignores her father's warnings about the shifting sand
dunes which threaten to swallow the village and tries to
sacrifice Singing Dog to the god, but the sand beats him
and the village is saved. A deep picture of early tribal life,
too complex for those for whom this is intended. Would
read aloud well.

IR 9+

330 The Shining Company

Bodley, 1990. 0 3703 1467 0
Red Fox, 1991. 0 0998 5580 1

Based on the Gododdin, the earliest surviving North British poem, and set in 600 A.D. when a band of warriors was
trained for a year in Dyn Eidin (Edinburgh), to fight the
Saxons. Told by Prosper, a shieldbearer, it tells of his friendship with Conn, his body servant, the training and battle,
and the last stand of the Shining Company. A story full of
the past, not just this particular part, but of those who went
before Prosper, and of the sight and sound of fighting men
preparing for battle.

IR 12+

331 Simon

Illustrated by Richard Kennedy
Oxford, 1957. o.p.

Simon joins Cromwell's Model Army during the Civil War,
but his closest friend, Amias, chooses to fight for the King.
Simon's travels with the army and his spell as a 'spy' are
well drawn, but the climax of the story is the testing of his
friendship with Amias. A fair portrayal of the Civil War in
the West Country, which is seen from Simon's side but not
unfairly so. One of the best books about the Civil War,
along with Hester Burton's *Kate Rider*.

IR 10+

332 Song for a Dark Queen

Pelham, 1978. o.p. 0 7207 1060 X

A sombre, violent story of Boudicca (Boadicea), told by her
harper Cadwan; briefly of her childhood, then of her love
for the man chosen to be her king, of the Romans' brutality
in dealing with her and her daughters, and of her time as
queen of the Iceni and the rising of the tribes against the
Romans. It is told in a suitably singing prose, occasionally
interspersed with letters from a Roman ADC to Suetonius

Paulinus. An interesting and heroic picture of the queen, full of tribal feeling.

IR 12+

333 Sun Horse, Moon Horse

Decorations by Shirley Felts
Bodley, 1977. o.p. 0 3703 0048 3
Red Fox, 1991. 0 0997 9560 4

Lubrin is the third son of a chieftain of the Iceni in Iron Age Britain. His gift is to be able to draw and he has a dream of taking his people to new horse runs. But the tribe is defeated by another and, as the price of his people's freedom, Lubrin creates the White Horse of Uffington and dies at the hand of the other chief. Beautiful rich prose constructs this idea of how the White Horse might have come to be.

IR 10+

334 The Truce of the Games

Illustrated by Victor Ambrus
Hamilton, 1971. o.p. 0 2410 2021 2 (Antelope)

Amyntas travels to Olympia for the Games and meets a Spartan boy. Although, Athens and Sparta are at war, a truce has been agreed for the duration of the Games. Amyntas and Leon become firm friends but their friendship is strongly tested during the race. A little too difficult for the age group for whom this series is intended, but would read aloud marvellously well.

IR 9+

335 Warrior Scarlet

Illustrated by Charles Keeping
Oxford, 1958. o.p.
Puffin, 1976. 0 1403 0895 4

Drem, who has a withered arm, fails his wolf slaying and cannot therefore achieve his warrior scarlet. He has to leave the tribe to live with the little Dark People and become a shepherd, but in the end meets his own wolf slaying with greater courage than he has needed before. Bronze Age Sussex is vividly recreated, and the theme of a boy coming to terms with his own disability is movingly told.

IR 10+

336 The Witch's Brat
Illustrated by Robert Micklewright
Oxford, 1970. o.p.
Red Fox, 1990. 0 0007 5080 5

Lovel, a misshapen boy, grandson of a healing woman, is cast out by his village, but uses the knowledge passed to him in working with Rahere, as he builds St Bartholomew's Hospital. (Rahere was a real person.) The details of healing at the time are effortlessly imparted in a rich evocation of the period.

IR 12+

Eve SUTTON

337 Green Gold
Illustrated by Paul Wright
Hamilton, 1976. o.p. 2418 9265 1 (Antelope)

Pioneering New Zealand is the setting for this story of an English boy who has become guardian of his father's treasure following his death on the voyage out. After many adventures he finds his uncle and is told the secret of the treasure – seeds! Told with warmth and humour.

IR 8+

338 Tuppenny Brown
Illustrated by Paul Wright.
Hamilton, 1977. o.p. 0 2418 9319 4 (Antelope)

A nicely turned story of a boy, deported to New Zealand to start a new life, finding his niche with a family and his vocation as a gardener/farmer. When the call comes to return to his old way of life, he finds the strength to reject it. Lovely drawings enhance this book.

IR 8+

From B.L. Picard, *One is One*

Robert SWINDELLS

339 **When Darkness Comes**
Hodder, 1973. o.p. 0 3401 7506 0

A stark tale of a primitive tribe divided by ambition, who find that to live in two small groups does not work and are united by an attack from another group. Life was a struggle to survive, and this gloom does rather permeate the story, but it is worth reading.

IR 10+

Geraldine SYMONS

340 The Rose Window
Illustrated by F.R. Exell
Heinemann, 1964. o.p.

In the first of the novels about Pansy Harcourt she is living with her grandfather and two aunts in a cathedral city in 1909. Pansy determines to find the pieces of the glass that formed the rose window in the cathedral which was defaced by Cromwell's soldiers. A warm and humourous vignette of Edwardian life, reminiscent of Gillian Avery.

IR 9+

341 The Quarantine Child
Illustrated by F.R. Exell
Heinemann, 1966. o.p.

In the sequel to *The Rose Window* Pansy is in quarantine for scarlet fever. She has met the redoubtable Atalanta, and it is to her she turns when she meets someone who needs help. A little sentimental, but still an enjoyable picture of Edwardian middle-class children.

IR 9+

342 The Workhouse Child
Illustrated by Alexy Pendle
Macmillan, 1969. o.p. 0 3330 3479 1

Pansy and her friend Atalanta are on holiday with Atalanta's grandmother on a farm by the sea. Pansy helps a workhouse child, but it all goes wrong and she runs away. A story told with humour and with some depth.

IR 9+

343 Miss Rivers and Miss Bridges
Illustrated by Alexy Pendle
Macmillan, 1971. o.p. 3331 2833 8

Pansy goes to stay with Atalanta in London and at last meets her unconventional parents. Atalanta leads her into the Suffragette movement and Pansy puts a brick through a window in Number 10 Downing Street. At a subsequent demonstration they are both arrested and taken to the cells. Some knowledge of the Suffragette movement is necessary to fully understand this story which because of the subject matter is deeper than the rest of this author's work.

IR 10+

344 Mademoiselle
Illustrated by Alexy Pendle
Macmillan, 1973. o.p. 3331 4494 1

In 1914 Pansy and Atalanta are staying in Paris with their friend Lydia at the British Embassy. Mademoiselle, who has chaperoned them across the Channel, arouses their suspicions and they track her believing she is a spy. There is a surprising end against the background of the outbreak of the First World War. Beautifully written with deep characterization.

IR 10+

Mildred C. TAYLOR

345 The Friendship and Other Stories
Gollancz, 1989. 0 5750 4495 0
Puffin, 1991. 0 1403 4615 5

These three powerful stories feature the Logans and are set in the southern states of America in the 1940s. In *The Friendship* they witness the shooting of a black man for using a white man's first name. Mildred Taylor has written from firsthand experience of segregation in strong, honest prose.

IR 9+

346 Roll of Thunder, Hear My Cry

Gollancz, 1977. 0 5750 2384 8
Puffin, 1988. 0 1403 2495 X (USA 1975, Newbery Medal 1976)

A magnificent story of a black family in Mississippi in 1930, told through Cassie, daughter of a landowning negro, who finds the injustice hard to bear and understand. Mama is a teacher and loses her job, Papa has his leg broken by some white men, but they refuse to stop fighting although the tragedy at the end is inevitable. A remarkable, unforgettable story.

IR 12+

347 Let the Circle be Unbroken

Gollancz, 1982. 0 5750 3084 4
Puffin, 1988. 0 1403 2558 (Plus) (U.S.A. 1980)

The sequel to *Roll of Thunder, Hear My Cry*, carries on the story of the Logan family. The dignity and pain of the proud family is told, taut and painful to read at times, in spare prose which describes life in a two-class system.

IR 12+

348 The Road to Memphis

Gollancz, 1990. 0 5750 4892 1 (USA 1990)

The third story, in which Cassie becomes involved in helping a friend who has hurt three white men after extreme provocation. Stacey, Cassie's brother, drives them to Memphis (not without incident) and they put Moe on the train to Chicago. A crystal clear picture of the difficulties faced by negroes in Mississippi just before the Second World War.

IR 12+

Theresa TOMLINSON

349 The Flither Pickers

Julia MacRae, 1990. 0 8620 3405 7
Walker, 1992. 0 7445 2043 6

In this stark tale of a fishing family in nineteenth-century northern England, Liza sees her grandmother die and her sister's fiancé drown. It is a picture of very close family life and of the strength of the women amongst them who launch the lifeboat when the men are at sea. Illustrated by contemporary photographs. A story with very limited appeal, but useful for local history. (Flithers are limpets).

IR 10+

John Rowe TOWNSEND

350 Dan Alone

Kestrel, 1983. o.p. 0 7226 5812 5

Poor Dan is shunted from person to person when his mother runs off. He lives rough with a family of thieves in the north of England during the Depression, until he eventually finds his own family. There is an interesting portrayal of anti-Semitism at the time. A sad, haunting story.

IR 10+

351 A Wish for Wings

Pictures by Philip Gough
Heinemann, 1973. o.p. 4349 4907 8 (Long Ago Children)

This tells of a boy who becomes apprenticed to Leonardo da Vinci and takes part in his experiments with a flying machine. Exciting and vivid, it gives a good idea of Leonardo's wide range of talents.

IR 7+

Mary TREADGOLD

352 Journey from the Heron
Cape, 1981. 0 2240 1970 8

In 1917, Betsy journeys to London to stay with Aunt Ba, befriends a German boy and feels the impact of the First World War. A difficult book to read because of the cockney dialect, but the class structure of the time comes through clearly enough, as does the proximity of the war, with Tom's gassing and the hospital at the Heron.

IR 10+

Geoffrey TREASE

353 The Baron's Hostage
Phoenix, 1952. o.p.
Brockhampton, 1973. o.p. (Revised edition) 0 3401 6864 1

Simon de Montfort and the events leading to the Battle of Evesham in 1265 form the background to this story of a young noble lad and a rich ward of King Henry III. The beginning of parliamentary rule in England is clearly described in a good adventure story which allows the history to be absorbed painlessly.

IR 10+

354 Bows Against the Barons
Brockhampton, 1966. o.p. (First published 1934)

Dickon kills a hart belonging to the king and, fearful of the punishment, runs away to Sherwood Forest, joins up with Robin Hood and becomes caught up in a peasant revolt against the barons. In this view of Robin Hood he is seen as the leader of an oppressed people, and the flavour of this 'revolution' comes over strongly with a good picture of peasant life and a political movement in embryo.

IR 10+

355 The Chocolate Boy
Illustrated by David Walker
Heinemann, 1975. o.p. 4349 4913 2 (Long Ago Children)

A short tale of a friendship between a country girl sent to
stay with a snobbish aunt, and a coloured slave boy in her
household. The boy escapes and Sarah returns home. The
illustrations mar a telling tale of the place of children in the
eighteenth century.

IR 7+

356 The Crown of Violet
Illustrated by C. Walter Hodges
Macmillan, 1952. o.p. 3330 3395 7

Alexis writes a play which is eventually produced and wins
the drama festival. This is an adventure story set in Ancient
Greece and peopled with real characters such as Socrates.
Some of the language does not ring true, for example, the
Thracian woman sounds as if she comes from Yorkshire but
the pace of the adventure story carries the reader along.

IR 10+

357 Cue for Treason
Blackwell, 1940. o.p.
Puffin, 1965. 0 1403 0231 X

Peter and Kit, fleeing the evil Sir Philip, take refuge with
Shakespeare's theatre company, become involved in Cecil's
Secret Service, and foil a plot against the Queen in a racy
adventure story, full of life in the Elizabethan theatre.

IR 10+

358 The Field of Forty Footsteps
Macmillan, 1977. o.p. 0 333 23070 1

After an uncertain beginning this story finds its feet when
the hero arrives in London to witness the restoration of the
theatre in the reign of Charles II. There is a good picture of

the theatre of the time, including the introduction of girls to play the female roles instead of boys.

IR 12+

359 Follow my Black Plume

Macmillan, 1963. o.p.

Mark and his tutor are caught up in Garibaldi's fight for the unification of Italy. The political background is well explained and the feel of a revolutionary army with its many factions is imparted. Most importantly of all the reader feels, part of the revolution and this brings the history alive. An outstanding book.

IR 12+

360 A Thousand for Sicily

Illustrated by Brian Wildsmith
Macmillan, 1964. o.p.

The sequel to *Follow my Black Plume* follows Mark in his participation in Garibaldi's journey to take Sicily for a united Italy. Vivid and real though this is, the reader would need to have read the first book to really understand the background. Despite a slightly implausible beginning, once into its stride this is a book worth reading.

IR 12+

361 The Hills of Varna

Illustrated by Teryer Evans
Macmillan, 1948. o.p.

A boy journeys across Europe in search of a Greek manuscript believed to be in the library of a hilltop monastery. There is much talk of Greek writers, of Erasmus and Copernicus in this readable adventure story set in spectacular scenery, with a heroine disguised as a boy (a favourite Trease device).

IR 10+

362 Horsemen on the Hills

Macmillan, 1971. o.p. 3331 2973 3

Sandro, a bastard, gets his chance of a good education and meets Caterina and Federigo, both of whom play a large part in his future. A good story set in Renaissance Italy, with much detail of the warring factions, education, Plato's theory of evolution and Platonic love. Federigo Sa Montefeltro was a real person.

IR 12+

363 The Iron Tsar

Macmillan, 1975. o.p. 3331 8653 2

An English lord rescues a dissident count in the Russia of Nicholas I. There is a good picture of tsarist Russia with its persecution, secret police and lack of personal freedom. Good characterization and Trease's expertise in making the reader feel the place make this an absorbing story.

IR 10+

364 A Masque for the Queen

Illustrated by Krystyna Turska
Hamilton, 1970. o.p. 2410 1872 2 (Antelope)

Elizabeth I comes to stay at Nick and Celia's house. They prepare a masque and also foil a plot to kill her. Vivid writing sweeps the young reader along and the illustrations catch the mood exactly.

IR 7+

365 Mist Over Athelney

Illustrated by R. S. Sherriffs and J. L. Stockle
Macmillan, 1958. o.p.

An English boy and girl make a journey to warn King Alfred of King Guthrun's treachery then join Alfred for his retreat to Athelney and his subsequent victory. This is not vintage Trease (the Danes are portrayed almost exclusively

From H. Burton, *Thomas*

as drunken thugs), but it is a good adventure set in a period not normally used.

IR 10+

366 Popinjay Stairs

Macmillan, 1973. o.p.
Pan Macmillan, 1993. 0 3303 2703 8 (The Popinjay Mystery)

Denzil Swift and Samuel Pepys attempt to get back the plans of Chatham defences when they are stolen in 1673 (an imaginary event). Denzil's entanglement with, and rescue of, a young lady playwright form part of the plot in a swashbuckling story set in London, giving a clear indication of the part the River Thames played in the life of the time.

IR 10+

367 The Red Towers of Granada

Illustrated by Charles Keeping
Macmillan, 1966. o.p.
Pan Macmillan, 1993. 0 3303 2628 7

In a powerful and dramatic opening a boy is found to have leprosy by the local priest and cast out from his village. He is 'cured' by a Jewish doctor and follows him across Europe from Nottingham to Toledo, Cordoba and Granada. This is a vivid and exciting adventure story which brings the eleventh century to life marvellously. One of Trease's best books, combining his favourite journey theme with his feel for place.

IR 10+

368 The Runaway Serf

Illustrated by Mary Russon
Hamilton, 1966. o.p. (Antelope)

A serf runs away and becomes apprenticed to a saddler in medieval York. He earns his freedom by being away for a year and a day. This brief, exciting story would be useful for older boys who are less able readers, because the hero is in his late teens.

IR 8+

369 The Seas of Morning

Illustrated by David Smee
Puffin, 1976. o.p.

Dick, a merchant's son, journeys from London to Rhodes to find out whether he would be suitable to join the Knights of St John. He rescues an English girl from Constantinople, and they return to Rhodes where they become involved in the siege of that island by the Turks in 1675. A well-written story with plenty to interest boys and girls, and with Trease's sense of place to the fore.

IR 10+

370 A Ship to Rome

Pictures by Leslie Atkinson
Heinemann, 1971. o.p. 4349 4904 3 (Long Ago Children)

Two children returning home to Rome from Alexandria with their mother try to free a slave boy. This brief story has an uninteresting start and would need introduction, but raises interesting points about slavery and freedom.

IR 9+

371 The Silken Secret

Illustrated by Alan Jessett
Blackwell, 1953. o.p.

The secret in the title is a method of making silken thread guarded jealously by the Italians, but which is discovered on a visit to Italy by Mr Mount. The orphaned hero, Dick, helps Mr Mount foil an attempt to kill him and destroy his mill. A good adventure story with a feel of place, and an unusual background.

IR 10+

372 Silver Guard

Illustrated by Alan Blyth
Blackwell, 1948. o.p.

An American boy comes to England to study medicine at the beginning of the Civil War. He stays with relations in Cumbria and then goes to Oxford, determined not to be drawn into the struggle, but eventually joins the Roundhead side and is involved in a siege of Silver Guard when the Cavalier villain is routed. At times a little stiff, this was one of the first books to take the Roundhead side in the conflict.

IR 10+

373 The Spy Catchers
Illustrated by Geoffrey Bargery
Hamilton, 1976. o.p. (Antelope)

Three children think they have overheard a French plot to invade England, but really it was William and Dorothy Wordsworth and Coleridge on a walking holiday and writing poetry. A difficult subject for the age group for whom this is intended, but could well be used as a short story with an older age range.

IR 10+

374 Thunder of Valmy
Illustrated by J.S. Goodall
Macmillan, 1960. o.p.

A boy from a poor family is adopted by an aristocratic lady in France at the time of the Revolution, and befriends a young aristocratic girl. As usual, Trease captures the spirit of a revolution, picturing the muddle and lack of decision. A fast-moving adventure story which details the causes of the French revolution and sympathizes with the poor.

IR 10+

375 When the Drums Beat
Illustrated by Janet Marsh
Heinemann, 1976. o.p. (Long Ago Children)

A family is divided by the Civil War, but the Roundhead father is hidden by the younger children and not given away by the Cavalier son. A vivid picture of how loyalties can divide and unite a family.

IR 7+

376 The White Nights of St Petersburg
Illustrated by William Stobbs
Macmillan, 1967. o.p.
R. Drew, 1987. 0 8626 7196 5 (Swallow)
Pan Macmillan, 1994. 0 3303 3423 9

The Russian revolution is seen though the eyes of a young American sent to St Petersburg by his father to learn about the Russians. He befriends a young, impressionable revolutionary and observes the confusing sequence of events. The flavour of a revolution is beautifully caught and the reader can envisage St Petersburg from the descriptions.

IR 10+

377 A Wood by Moonlight and Other Stories
Chatto, 1981. o.p. 0 7011 2575 6

Many of these stories appeared elsewhere and show Trease's mastery of the medium. Nine of the twelve are historical (two of them set in the Second World War). A good collection to read aloud.

IR 9+

378 Word to Caesar
Illustrated by Geoffrey Whittam
Macmillan, 1956. o.p.

This adventure story of a boy's quest to help an exiled Roman poet ranges from Roman Britain to the Emperor Hadrian's Rome. There is a spirited heroine, Trease's favourite journey theme, and many details of Roman life.

IR 10+

Henry TREECE

379 **The Bombard**
Illustrated by Christine Price
Bodley Head, 1959. o.p.

A young knight, who fought with the Black Prince at Crecy, returns to the Welsh Marches to save his inheritance. In Calais he had been tasked to make the bombards (early cannon), and he uses this knowledge to regain his sister and land. Glimpses of the troubles in Wales and France form the background to this swashbuckling story.

IR 9+

380 **The Bronze Sword**
Illustrated by Mary Russon
Hamilton, 1965. o.p. (Antelope)

A retired Roman soldier is threatened by Boadicea on his farm, then offered friendship and the sword of the title by her nephew. A magnificent story, warm and deep, which would read aloud well to all ages.

IR 9+

381 **The Children's Crusade**
Illustrated by Christine Price
Bodley Head, 1958; new edition 1971. o.p. 0 3700 1222 4

Based on the facts of the Children's Crusade of 1212, this tells of Alys and Stephen from a noble French family, who follow Stephen de Cloyes only to become slaves. They escape but are captured again and then rescued by their father's old friend. Deep characterization helps the rather stiff story along.

IR 10+

382 **The Dream-Time**
With a postscript by Rosemary Sutcliff
Illustrated by Charles Keeping
Brockhampton, 1967. o.p. 3400 4050 5

An impressionistic novel of man at different periods of pre-history, giving a good picture of warring tribes and a figure who would rather live peaceably. Produced in a format which suggests a young readership, but more suitable for older children.

IR 10+

383 The Eagles Have Flown
Illustrated by Christine Price
Bodley, 1954. o.p. 3700 1210 0

After his parents's death Festus joins Artos the Bear and follows him to the Battle of Dublas. The story ends with Arthur's killing by Medrault at Camlan, which Treece makes into an assassination. An interesting portrayal of Arthur, who appears more barbaric than heroic.

IR 10+

384 The Golden One
Illustrated by William Stubbs
Bodley, 1961. o.p.

Set in 1204 and the years following, this is the story of Constantine and Theodora, children of the Norse captain of the Varangian Guard in Byzantium. When the Franks come the children become part of the confused struggle for power, and after escaping, eventually end up with Genghis Khan. Difficult reading, partly because of the complex political background, but an interesting picture of a less than civilized world.

IR 12+

385 Horned Helmet
Illustrated by Charles Keeping
Brockhampton, 1963. o.p.

Beautiful prose tells the story of Beorn who, having lost his father, is rescued by the man who becomes his foster-father. The growth of their relationship is well drawn against the background of Viking life. Set in Iceland and northern England, this gives a good picture of the Viking ethos and way of life. The tremendous illustrations by Charles Keeping add enormously to the story.

IR 8+

386 Hounds of the King
Illustrated by Christine Price
Bodley, 1955. o.p. 0 3700 1221 6

Beornoth joins the House Carles, the soldiers who form the King's bodyguard, and follows Harold Godwinson to Hastings where Harold is killed in a last stand with his Carles about him. The romance and drama of the battle for the kingship are movingly told.

IR 10+

387 The Invaders: Three Stories
Introduced by Margery Fisher and illustrated by Charles Keeping
Brockhampton, 1972. o.p. 0 3401 4764 4

The first of these stories deals with the relationship of a Roman soldier with a tribal chieftain in Britain, the second with a band of marauding Vikings and the third with a House Carle of Harold's who vows to kill William but finds he cannot. They show Treece's mastery of these periods and would read aloud splendidly.

IR 9+

388 The Last of the Vikings
Illustrated by Charles Keeping
Brockhampton, 1964. o.p. 0 3401 3485 2

Harald Hardrada looks back from the Battle of Stamford Bridge over past episodes in his life. This is told in Treece's 'saga' style which suits the subject exactly, a stately prose full of heroic deaths and pronouncements, which would read aloud or dramatize so well.

IR 10+

From B.L. Picard, *One is One*

389 Legions of the Eagle
Illustrated by Christine Price
Bodley, 1954. o.p. 0 3700 0920 7
Puffin, 1970. 0 1403 0247 6

A Belgae boy, who witnessed the death of his father at the Battle of Camulodunum when Caratacus faced the Romans, is captured and sent to Gaul to be a slave to a centurion's son. They become friends and return to Britain, searching for their parents to find the Romans in full command. The contrast between the ordered life of the Romans and the barbaric life of the tribes is well made.

IR 10+

390 Man with a Sword
Decorations by William Stobbs
Bodley, 1962. o.p.

Hereward is a simple man giving his loyalty to one person after another only to find this trust abused. His relationship with William the Conqueror is realistically told, and Hereward's intrinsic dignity in the midst of a barbaric world comes through. In his introduction Treece states that he has reconstructed Hereward's life from the few details known. This is a difficult, but interesting read.

IR 12+

391 The Queen's Brooch
Hamilton, 1966. o.p.

A Roman tribune is involved in Boadicea's uprising and defeat at the hands of the Romans led by Suetonius. The beautiful prose gives a dignity and power to the story, and this stands well alongside Rosemary Sutcliff's stories about the Romans. It is clearly seen how the Roman army was made up of many races, and how barbaric some of the tribes were.

IR 10+

392 Splintered Sword
Illustrated by Charles Keeping
Brockhampton, 1965. o.p. 0 3401 3406 0

A chance encounter leads an orphan boy in the Orkneys at the end of the eleventh century to try the Viking way of life. However, he finds it hard and unsatisfying and, after some searching, finds the father figure he needs in a Norman soldier. A gloomy and sad story, portraying the end of an era and a boy's heartbreaking search for any warmth in his life. Charles Keeping's violent illustrations add to the atmosphere.

IR 9+

393 Swords from the North
Faber, 1967. o.p. 5710 8136 3

The epic story of Harald Hardrada's time as Captain of the Byzantine Emperor's Varangian Guard in 1034–44 is based on the Saga of the Norse Kings written between 1223 and 1235 by Snorri Sturlson. It portrays the trials and strain of leadership and the power struggles within the Byzantine empire. This is Treece at the height of his powers and in his favourite period.

IR 12+

394 Viking's Dawn
Illustrated by Christine Price
Bodley, 1955. o.p.

Harald Sigurdson goes with his father to find another lord to serve, and discovers Thorkell about to sail in his new longship. His father is wounded, so he sails alone and Thorkell becomes his 'father'. They sail to plunder, but in the end are shipwrecked and captured and in the subsequent escape only Harald survives to return to the village. The first in the saga of the three stories, this is a little stiff to begin but once into its stride is a stirring tale of the Vikings, explaining much about their brotherhood and ethos.

IR 10+

395 The Road to Miklagard
Illustrated by Christine Price
Bodley, 1957. o.p.

The second story follows Harald's journeys to Ireland, Spain and thence to Miklagard. It does read rather more like a fairy tale than history as he meets giants, finds treasure, and so forth.

IR 10+

396 Viking's Sunset
Illustrated by Christine Price
Bodley, 1960. o.p.

The third story, in which an older Harald sails, to avenge the pillaging of his village. He journeys to Iceland, Greenland and then the land of the red men where he meets his end as foretold in the early part of the book. A sad and heroic tale.

IR 10+

The three stories above (Nos 394–6) are published together as *The Viking Saga*
Puffin, 1985. 0 1403 1791 0

397 War Dog
Illustrated by Roger Payne
Brockhampton, 1969. o.p. 0 3400 3940 X

Bran, a war dog at the time of Caratacus, takes part in the Battle of Camulodunum where he is wounded and captured by the Gauls. He is rescued and nursed back to health by a Roman tribune, takes part in the attack on Mai Dun and retires to Ostia at the end. An unusual and accessible story, full of battles but also of warmth and love.

IR 8+

J. TULLY

398 The Raven and the Cross
Illustrated by Derek Collard
BBC, 1974. o.p. 0 5631 2472 5

Edwina sees her father slain in the manor at Chippenham he held from King Alfred. She manages to join the King with useful knowledge of Viking movements and is responsible for Alfred's surprise for the Vikings (historical licence). A spirited reconstruction of events at Edington, first written for 'Merry-go-round'.

IR 8+

Philip TURNER

399 Steam on the Line
Illustrated by Trevor Ridley
Oxford, 1968. o.p. 1927 1284 5

Taffy, son of the carpenter, and Sarah, his neighbour and friend, witness plans to sabotage the railway by the owner of the coach company. Their courage and resolution save the day and they are suitably rewarded. The high feelings at the coming of the railway are not hidden in this warm story.

IR 9+

Kenneth ULYATT

400 North Against the Sioux
Collins, 1965. o.p.

Based on fact, this tells of one year in the life of a frontier fort established on Indian land, and of the great fight to keep it. A fair and balanced account putting the Indian's case well in an exciting and well-written story.

IR 12+

Hilda VAN STOCKUM

401 The Winged Watchman
Farrar, Straus and Girous, 1988. o.p.
0 5711 2100 4 (USA 1962)

Dirk, Jan and Joris of the Verhagen family become involved in the Resistance movement in the Netherlands, while Father has an unelectrified polder mill which he can keep going to save the crops and help the community to survive. The slightly American prose does not mar a tale of courage and resistance.

IR 9+

Jill Paton WALSH

402 The Butty Boy
Illustrated by Juliette Palmer
Macmillan, 1975. o.p.
Puffin, 1986. 0 1403 1962 X

Harriet runs away, almost by mistake, and helps on a canal boat to take the cargo for a man who would lose the contract if the deadline is not met. Told in flashback, the contrast between Harriet's life and that of Ned and Bess is clearly drawn. Good illustrations capture the mood and period.

IR 8+

403 The Dolphin Crossing

Macmillan, 1967. o.p. 3330 9096 9
Puffin, 1970. 0 1403 0457 6

A telling story of a friendship between two boys of very different classes who come together to help evacuate British soldiers from Dunkirk in the *Dolphin* of the title. The class distinction is clearly seen between the Cockney evacuee and the son of the big house. A good novel, made particularly fine by the depth of the characterization.

IR 10+

404 The Emperor's Winding Sheet

Macmillan, 1974. o.p. 3331 5533 5

The fall of Emperor Constantine at Constantinople is seen through the eyes of a young man. Beautiful descriptions of the city and the way of life are interspersed with the complex reasons for Constantine's position with the Greek and Roman church, making this an almost adult book.

IR 14+

405 Fireweed

Macmillan, 1969. o.p. 3310 6180 0
Puffin, 1972. 0 1403 0560 2

Bill, a lonely evacuee from London to Wales, returns to London and meets Julia who has escaped being evacuated to Canada. They live rough together in the London of the Blitz experiencing the full horror of the raids. Eventually Julia becomes ill and they are parted. A sad story of the chaos of war and of the class differences of the time.

IR 12+

406 Grace

Viking, 1991. 0 6708 3820 9

A fictionalized account of the dramatic events which made Grace Darling a heroine, and of the effect upon her life afterwards. Grace herself tells the story of the night she aided her father to rescue the survivors of the *Forfarshire*, and of the bitterness and hostility towards her after the event. Skilful use of language makes this a vivid and sobering experience.

IR 12+

407 A Parcel of Patterns
Kestrel, 1983. 0 6708 0861 X
Puffin, 1988. 0 1403 2627 8 (Plus)

Based on fact, this tells of the coming of the plague to the village of Eyam in Derbyshire in the seventeenth century, and in particular how Mall and her Thomas dealt with the horrifying events. A sombre story told in beautiful stylized language which would lend itself well to dramatizing.

IR 12+

408 The Walls of Athens
Illustrated by David Smee
Heinemann, 1977. o.p. 4349 4931 0 (Long Ago Children)

An Athenian boy runs with a message to Sparta and helps save Athens from attack until the city is prepared. Beautifully written although a little stiff, this would need introducing to children as the political background is complex.

IR 9+

Jill Paton WALSH, and Kevin CROSSLEY-HOLLAND

409 Wordhoard: Anglo-Saxon Stories
Macmillan, 1969. o.p. 0 3331 0237 1

Eight short stories set before 1066 depicting various aspects of life at the time. Told in a stylized prose which requires perseverance but the rhythm of which the reader gradually acquires, they would need introduction, but would read aloud well.

IR 12+

James WATSON

410 The Freedom Tree
Gollancz, 1976; revised edition 1986. o.p. 0 5750 3779 2

Will, whose father has died in the early days of the Spanish Civil War, joins the International Brigade with a band of people he meets along the way. He drives ambulances and carries stretchers, seeing his friends die. He is captured, escapes, and makes his way to Guernica where he witnesses the destruction of the city. The story gathers depth as it progresses and becomes a moving account.

IR 14+

Ronald WELCH

411 Bowman of Crecy
Illustrated by Ian Ribbons
Oxford, 1966. o.p.

Hugh Fletcher and his well-trained band of outlaws are offered a place in the Company of Sir John Carey to fight the French for Edward III. There are graphic accounts of the subsequent battles culminating with the Battle of Crecy. The incident at the ford is based on fact, although the name of Hugh Le Despenser is not used. Welch was a military historian and all his books are full of details of weapons and battles which make them live.

IR 10+

From R. Sutcliff, *The Silver Branch*

412 Captain of Dragoons

Illustrated by William Stobbs
Oxford, 1956. o.p.

Charles Carey, a captain in the Dragoon Guards, is sent to
spy in the courts of the Pretender, James Stuart, and Louis
XIV. Set against Marlborough's campaign which culminates
in the Battle of Blenheim, this is a swashbuckling story
with plenty of duels and swordfights as well as battles.

IR 12+

413 Captain of Foot

Illustrated by William Stobbs
Oxford, 1959. o.p.

The exploits of Christopher Carey in this book are partly
based on those of Tom Hopkins. Christopher takes part in
Wellington's campaigns in the Peninsular Wars. There are
vivid descriptions of army life and the battles, although
Christopher himself is not a swordsman and is undecided
about an army career.

IR 12+

414 Ensign Carey

Oxford, 1976. o.p. 0 1927 1386 8

William Carey is sent down from Cambridge and joins the
Indian Army as an ensign in the 84th Bengal Native Infan-
try. The climax of the story is a graphic description of the
Indian Mutiny of 1857 and it ends in William's ignomini-
ous death while trying to escape with loot. The causes of
the Mutiny are clearly drawn, and details of the lives of the
English in India are well described.

IR 12+

415 Escape from France

Illustrated by William Stobbs
Oxford, 1960. o.p.

Richard Carey is sent by his father and uncle to rescue a distant relative, a Marquis, from the French Revolution. The events are seen from the aristocratic side in an adventure story, that differs from Welch's other work in that it does not deal with battles.

IR 12+

416 For the King
Illustrated by William Stobbs
Oxford, 1969. o.p. 0 1927 7051 9 (Oxford Children's Library)

The story of Neil Carey who fought for Charles I in the Civil War, this is a fair and interesting account showing how the war was brought about by fanatics on both sides. The detailed stories of battles become rather difficult to follow from time to time.

IR 12+

417 The Galleon
Illustrated by Victor Ambrus
Oxford, 1971. o.p. 0 1927 1324 8

Robert Penderyn falls into a seafaring life as the result of a duelling accident, and another accident with the rapier in Spain makes for his imprisonment and subsequent escape from a Spanish castle. This swashbuckling story ends with a plot to capture Mary, Queen of Scots. Full of technical details of seafaring life, an enjoyable and racy story.

IR 10+

418 The Hawk
Illustrated by Gareth Floyd
Oxford, 1967. o.p.

The Earl of Aubigny, a privy councillor to Elizabeth I, builds a galleon (the 'Hawk' of the title), which he hopes will capture Spanish shipping and in which his son Harry sails. Various historical figures appear – among them Drake, Elizabeth I and Walsingham who invokes Harry's help in a (fictitious) plot by Mary Stuart against Elizabeth.

There are detailed descriptions of life at sea and the illustrations are superb, particularly the double spread of a galleon on p.136.

IR 10+

419 Knight Crusader

Illustrated by William Stobbs
Oxford, 1954. o.p. (Carnegie Medal 1954)

Philip D'Aubigny fights against Saladin, is captured, escapes and fights the Infidel again with Richard I. He then returns to England to claim his inheritance of the castle at Llansteplan. The complicated political background of the Crusades is well explained and the vivid details of military life meticulously described; the reader will feel the heat of the sun on his back in this quite outstanding story.

IR 12+

420 Mohawk Valley

Illustrated by William Stobbs
Oxford, 1958. o.p.

Alan Carey is accused of cheating and sent down from Cambridge. His father packs him off to America, where he manages the family estates, becomes a part-time soldier and eventually helps General Wolfe scale the Heights of Abraham and defeat the French. The stigma of cheating is removed from his name and he settles in America. A good story, lacking only a female figure to round it off, which gives good details of pioneering life.

IR 10 +

421 Nicholas Carey

Illustrated by William Stobbs
Oxford, 1963. o.p.

An unwilling soldier, Nicholas is caught up first with Italian revolutionaries and then in the Siege of Sebastopol in the Crimean war. A good picture of life in a regiment at the time showing how officers bought their commissions and promotion.

IR 12+

422 Sun of York

Illustrated by Doreen Roberts
Oxford, 1970. o.p. 0 1927 1315 9

Owen Lloyd, son of a knight, is caught up in the power struggle between the Lancastrians and the Yorkists in 1469-71. Descriptions of battles and fighting form the greater part of this book in which several historical figures appear, principally the Duke of Gloucester (afterwards Richard III). The depth of characterization alleviates the savageness of the politics and the battles.

IR 10+

423 Tank Commander

Illustrated by Victor Ambrus
Oxford, 1972. o.p.

A vivid and crowded story telling of Lt. Carey's experiences in the First World War, mainly in the trenches, but also witnessing the introduction of the tank into modern warfare. The great amount of military detail seems to make the characters a little shadowy, but it is a good story showing the horror of the conflict.

IR 12+

424 Zulu Warrior

Illustrated by David Harris
David & Charles, 1974. o.p. 0 7153 6555 X

Robert Manyan is sent to South Africa where he takes part in the Zulu Wars of 1879. The story is based on the facts of the Battle of Rorke's Drift and shows quite clearly how unprepared the British Army was for this sort of warfare, but also how courageous it was.

IR 12+

Robert WESTALL

425 Blitzcat

Macmillan, 1989. o.p. 0 3334 7499 6

Pan, 1990. 0 3303 1040 2 (Piper)

Lord Gort, a female cat, goes looking in wartime Britain for her master, a pilot who has gone missing. She journeys across England meeting various characters along the way – Sergeant Smith, Ollie, Susan and Mrs Semple – until she finds her master. Using his favourite cat theme, Westall evokes the atmosphere of wartime superbly well.

IR 14+

426 The Machine Gunners

Macmillan, 1975. o.p. 0 3331 8644 3

Puffin, 1977. 0 1403 0973 X

(Carnegie Medal 1975)

Chas finds a machine gun in the wreckage of a Luftwaffe plane, rescues it and, with his friends, builds a fortress in Nicky's Anderson shelter to have a go at the Germans. A brilliant evocation of wartime Newcastle and of the fever war engenders, even in children. Told in sometimes rough language, this is a vibrant story with great appeal.

IR 10+

427 Fathom Five

Macmillan, 1979. 0 3332 7385 0

Puffin, 1982. 0 1403 1353 2

Two years have passed since *The Machine Gunners* and Chas McGill finds a floating radio beacon to pinpoint positions for U-boats. With Cem, Audrey and Sheila, he tries to track down the spy in Garmouth. The four get mixed up in the seamier side of port life and find people are not always what they seem. Tragedy and humour live side by side in this well-written story with its laconic dialogue.

IR 12+

428 **Kingdom by the Sea**
Methuen, 1990. 0 3743 4205 9

Harry, convinced after a bombing raid that his parents are dead, goes on the run befriended by a dog. He journeys up the Northumbrian coast having to keep on the move to avoid being detected and taken into care. There is a totally unexpected ending to this fine story of a boy's courage.

IR 10+

Laura Ingalls WILDER

429 **Little House in the Big Woods**
Illustrated by Garth Williams
Methuen, 1956. 0 4160 7130 9
Puffin, 1963. 0 1403 0194 1 (USA 1932)

In this, the first of the series, Laura is five years old and lives in a log cabin in the woods in the Wisconsin of the 1880s. The book is full of the domestic details of life, the chores to be done and the supplying and preparation of food; Pa entertaining the family in the evening with songs; cosy and warm, as befits the story of a five year old. The sequence of stories is based on Laura Ingalls Wilder's own life and makes an impressive achievement.

IR 7+

430 **Little House on the Prairie**
Illustrated by Garth Williams
Methuen, 1937. 0 1460 7140 6
Puffin, 1964. 0 1403 0204 2 (USA 1935)

In the second story Ma and Pa and the family leave Wisconsin in a covered wagon and move on to settle on the prairie. The intimate details of their daily life and the warmth of the family are lovingly portrayed, but the difficulties of the life are not disguised. Eventually the government orders all the settlers out and they have to move on.

IR 8+

431 **On the Banks of Plum Creek**
Illustrated by Garth Williams
Methuen, 1958. 0 4160 7150 3
Puffin, 1965. 0 1403 0228 X (USA 1953)

The family move to live in a dugout on the banks of Plum
Creek and Pa begins to farm. He buys the timber for the
house on credit and builds a house, but the wheat crop fails
because of grasshoppers and he has to go East to look for
work. The girls go to school and survive the grasshopper
invasion and the severe winter. Laura's growth has to be
matched by the reader in a story which does not hide the
harshness and fragility of their existence.

IR 9+

432 **By the Shores of Silver Lake**
Illustrated by Garth Williams
Lutterworth 1961. 0 7188 0128 8
Puffin, 1967. 0 1403 0303 0 (USA 1939)

Laura continues to grow up in this story of the move West
where Pa gets a job with the railroad, and the new town is
built along with the homestead. The hardship of life is not
glossed over, but the minutiae of everyday existence is
chronicled, the endless housework and supply and preparation of food. Through it all comes the warmth of family
life, the strength of the Wilder marriage, and the support
given and received by friends.

IR 10+

433 **The Long Winter**
Illustrated by Garth Williams
Lutterworth, 1962. 7188 0520 8 (USA 1940)
Puffin, 1968. 0 1403 0381 2

The cold of the long winter in the prairie town really creeps
through this story of the seven-month winter the family
survived. The intense cold and the awful blizzards come
vividly to life for the reader, and the details of the monoto-
nous diet and the lethargy cold brings are clearly drawn.

Almanzo Wilder makes a substantial appearance in this story. Perhaps the best of the series, although it is difficult to separate the one from the whole.

IR 10+

434 Little Town on the Prairie
Illustrated by Garth Williams
Lutterworth, 1963. 0 7188 0519 4
Puffin, 1969. 0 1403 0417 7 (USA 1941)

Laura is now fourteen and gets a job in town but carries on going to school in order to be able to get her teaching certificate, so that she can keep Mary at the College for the Blind in Iowa. Full of details of life in the Dakota of the 1880s.

IR 10+

From R. Sutcliff, *The Shield Ring*

435 Farmer Boy

Illustrated by Garth Williams
Lutterworth, 1965. 0 7188 0298 5 (USA 1933)
Puffin, 1972. 0 1403 0568 8

Almanzo's stable upbringing on a farm in New York State contrasts with Laura's peripatetic childhood. The Wilders lived well and ate a lot, judging by this story which dwells a lot on food. Schooling played second fiddle to the farm work, and Almanzo's dream to have a colt of his own to break in is realized. An interesting story which completes the picture.

IR 9+

436 These Happy Golden Years

Illustrated by Garth Williams
Lutterworth, 1963. 0 7188 0918 1
Puffin, 1970. 0 1403 0461 (USA 1943)

At fifteen Laura goes away for two months to teach school. It is an unhappy existence and only Almanzo's coming to collect her to bring her home makes it bearable. Gradually their relationship develops, gently by today's standards, and the story ends with their marriage. A warm, detailed story of community life, simple but good and dominated by the prairie.

IR 10+

437 The First Four Years

With an epilogue by Rose Wilder Lane
Lutterworth, 1973. o.p.
Puffin, 1978. 0 1403 1028 2 (USA 1971)

A slight story giving a different slant on the series, in which Laura and Almanzo cope with the ruination of crop after crop and the loss of their baby son. Rose Wilder Lane, their daughter, adds an epilogue which fills in the details of their life. Interesting to read as a postscript to the novels.

IR 12+

Barbara WILLARD

The Mantlemass Novels

The following eight books (Nos 438–45) comprise what are known as the Mantlemass novels and are Barbara Willard's great contribution to historical fiction for children. Listed as they were written, rather than in strict chronological order, they cover the years between the death of Richard III and the end of the Civil War.

438 The Lark and the Laurel

Drawings by Gareth Floyd
Longman, 1970. o.p. 0 5821 5852 4
Macdonald, 1987. 0 3561 3169 6

Cecily Jolland is left with her aunt at Mantlemass in Ashdown Forest, Sussex, when her father leaves for France after the death of Richard III. Here she finds a new way of life, shown by Dame Elizabeth. She is haunted by a dream she cannot quite remember, but in time, and with her meeting with Lewis Mallory, all becomes clear. The details of daily life in the forest with its iron furnaces and farms are beautifully drawn in this outstanding book.

IR 10+

439 The Sprig of Broom

Decorations by Paul Shordlaw
Longman, 1971. o.p. 0 5821 5854 0

Medley Plashet knows he and his father are different from other people, but only when his father leaves and Medley follows does he discover his secret, that he is the bastard grandson of Richard III and his father has been protecting him from the men who sought to make him a Pretender to the throne. Around this story the community of Mantlemass is depicted going on with its daily life. Medley's acceptance of his heritage but rejection of its misuse is well portrayed.

IR 10+

440 A Cold Wind Blowing
Longman, 1972. o.p. 0 5821 5855 9
Macdonald, 1988. 0 3561 3172 6

Against the background of the Dissolution of the monasteries, Dick Plashet's second son meets Isabella and experiences happiness and tragedy. The life of Ghylls Hatch and Mantlemass carries on and Piers is received home again. The story shows clearly how the great events outside did touch the lives of ordinary people, like ripples on a pond.

IR 10+

441 The Iron Lily
(First published 1973)
Macdonald, 1988. 0 3561 3178 5
Macdonald, 1988. 0 3561 3179 3
(Guardian Award 1974)

An older woman is the heroine of this, the fourth in the series. Lilias Rowan is born with the crooked shoulder handed down from Richard III, and only discovers after her mother's death that her name was Medley. She marries an iron master and when he dies she takes on the foundry. In time she becomes respected as the Master. A powerful story of a woman coming to terms with herself only through a near tragedy.

IR 12+

442 Harrow and Harvest
(First published 1974)
Macdonald, 1989. 0 3561 3180 7
Macdonald, 1989. 0 3561 3181 5

Edmund Medley fulfils his father's dying wish by going to Mantlemass, but his arrival causes consternation because he is a Royalist. Nicholas Highwood, Master, teaches Edmund a great deal but eventually leaves with his wife for the New World. Cecilia stays with her love and Edmund meets a tragic end, but the story ends on a note of hope of rebuilding. Again this shows clearly the effect of great events on the lives of ordinary people.

IR 12+

443 The Eldest Son

(First published 1980)
Macdonald, 1988. 0 3561 3174 2
Macdonald, 1988. 0 3561 3175 0

Harry Medley does not have the love of horses of the rest of his family, and overruling his brother while his father is away, brings tragedy and ruin to Ghylls Hatch. The strength of his marriage holds him together while he makes the painful decision to go his own way. This story of a conflict of wills between father and son makes unpleasant reading at times and requires maturity to understand.

IR 12+

444 A Flight of Swans

(First published 1980)
Macdonald, 1988. 0 3561 3176 9
Macdonald, 1988. 0 3561 3177 7

This tells the story of Ursula Medley, a few years after her marriage to Robin, of the failure of that marriage, and her relationship with Roger Jolland, a distant cousin with whose father she falls in love. A story of tragedy, betrayal and love, showing how bitterness can destroy a man. Rich in the feel of the countryside and the closeness of the Mantlemass community.

IR 12+

445 The Keys of Mantlemass

(First published 1980)
Macdonald, 1989. 0 3561 3182 2
Macdonald, 1988. 0 3561 3183 1

These stories bridge the gaps in the tapestry woven by the author in previous novels, and cover the years 1485–1644, telling of the descendants of John Verrall and Cecilia Highwood, and the Medleys who went to the New World.

IR 12+

446 Augustine Came to Kent

Illustrated by Hans Guggenheim
World's Work, 1964. o.p.

Augustine's mission to England is seen through the eyes of a British boy who is taken to Rome with his father as a slave and then befriended by Pope Gregory. At times this is a moving account of conversion.

IR 9+

447 The Country Maid

Hamilton, 1978. o.p. 0 2418 9936 2

Cassie goes to the Garsides as a maid of all work in the 1930s. She has come from the country, is only sixteen and full of admiration for Jean Garside (all of eighteen!). Jean and Cassie help each other, but eventually Cassie returns home to the boy she left behind. A sympathetic portrait of a girl growing up, told partly through the medium of Jean's diary, but coloured with telling details of class and differing conditions of living.

IR 10+

448 The Farmer's Boy

Julia MacRae, 1991. 1 85681 140 9

Farmer Hoad wants to hand the tenancy of his farm to Harry, but the landlord has other plans. Against this background the work of the farm has to go on, and Harry has to fit in his schooling round it. Nineteenth-century farming with the difficulties of tenant farmers and the power of the landlords is well described.

IR 12+

449 The Grove of Green Holly

Illustrated by Gareth Floyd
Constable, 1967. o.p.

Rafe, son and grandson of an actor (a forbidden profession
in Cromwellian England), flees with his family to his grandfather's haven, a grove of green holly in Ashdown Forest.
Here Rafe finds work as a smith and has to make a decision
about his future as news of the King's return reaches the
forest. A deep story with good characterization and an interesting picture of the bigotry of Puritan England.

IR 10+

450 Hetty

Illustrated by Pamela Mason
Constable, 1962. o.p.

Spirited Hetty Jebb finds a good friend in Blanche Verity
even though the Veritys are a station above the Jebbs who
own a shop. Set in Victorian Brighton this is full of the
small details of the life of a middle-class Victorian child.

IR 9+

451 The Miller's Boy

Illustrated by Gareth Floyd
Kestrel, 1976. o.p. 0 7226 5073 6

A sideshoot from the Mantlemass novels in that this tells the
story of Thomas Welfare who gave Lewis Mallory his red
hat. Thomas is the miller's grandson and befriends Lewis
when the latter comes to live at Ghylls Hatch. The friendship
has to end because they come from different classes. A deceptively simple story of two boys sharing a good time against
the background of the lives of the forest people.

IR 9+

452 Ned Only

Julia MacRae, 1985. 0 8620 3197 4

Set just before the Great Fire of London, this is a romance in
the great tradition viewed by Ned Only, turnspit boy in the

household of Sir Joshua Bidgood. Sir Joshua hopes to marry his rich niece to a rich title, but she falls in love with the tutor to his son. Ned is an accomplice to their elopement in a charming tale of love.

IR 12+

453 **Priscilla Pentecost**
Illustrated by Doreen Roberts
Hamilton, 1970. o.p. (Antelope)

Priscilla lives a hard, but not unhappy, life with Farmer Balcombe. Her guardian from the Parish decides he can give her a better life and sends her to be a companion to a spoilt little girl, but Priscilla is very unhappy and runs away. A telling tale of differences between children, rich and poor, enchantingly told.

IR 7+

454 **The Queen of the Pharisee's Children**
Julia MacRae, 1983. 0 8620 3148 6
Walker, 1989. 0 7445 1310 3

Will is the son of a tinker family in the days of Cromwell. His mother Moll (called the Queen of the Pharisees) divides her family unknowingly when the family fall foul of the vagrancy laws, and Will goes to live in the only house he's ever known. Slowly this becomes his way of life, and when he sees his parents again he finds he is no longer willing or able to live as they do. Set in Ashdown Forest and full of the countryside, this is a moving experience.

IR 12+

455 **The Ranger's Daughter**
Julia MacRae, 1992. 1 8568 1262 6

Lucy's sister Ellen goes from her father's forestry cottage to be a maid at Brackfield Place and Lucy finds it hard to be alone, yet she loves the forest. Her father becomes Head Ranger and gets involved in quartering the forest for game, while she observes the romance between Mr Edward and the governess. A quiet story set in the nineteenth century, beautifully told and full of the countryside.

IR 12+

Ursula Moray WILLIAMS

456 The Noble Hawks
Hamilton, 1959. o.p.

Dickon, a yeoman's son, wants above all to be a falconer and by luck is given the chance. This is somewhat dated now, but worth reading for its picture of falconry and life in a medieval castle.

IR 10+

Barbara Ker WILSON

457 The Lovely Summer
Illustrated by Marina Hoffer
Constable, 1960. o.p.
Chivers, 1972. 8 5594 696 2

Vanessa and Helen grow into womanhood against the background of the Suffragette movement and the cloud of the approach of the First World War. The differing ways in which suffragettes viewed their fight are made clear, and the place of women is deftly pointed out.

IR 12+

Sylvia WOODS

458 Drover's Dog
Illustrated by Gavin Rowe
Faber, 1983. o.p. 0 571 1193 X

A drover's dog is left to find his own way home from London to Bridgwater, as was the custom. But he is only a pup and William is worried so he sets off to find him. A charming and unusual story set against the background of the early troubles with the King at the beginning of the Civil War.

IR 9+

Richard WORMSER

459 Ride a Northbound Horse
Oxford, 1964. o.p.

Cav, orphaned and on his way to Texas, is befriended by Big Cav. He tries school, but leaves to join the herd drive to Texas. Cav's journey, his acceptance by the cowboys and the warm companionship of Big Cav are well described in terse prose. Good to read aloud, particularly to boys who are less able readers. Set in the late nineteenth century.

IR 9+

Alki ZEI

460 Wildcat Under Glass
Translated from the Greek by Edward Fenton
Gollancz, 1969. o.p. 0 5750 0257 3 (Greece 1963)

Greece acquires a dictator Metaxas, not to the liking of Myrto and Melissa's grandfather, and even less to that of Niko, their cousin. He becomes a freedom fighter and

Melissa helps him with messages. The political background would need explaining, but the book is exciting and interesting. Set just before the Second World War.

IR 9+

461 **Petros' War**
Translated from the Greek by Edward Fenton
Gollancz, 1972. o.p. 0 5750 1563 2

Petros becomes gradually involved with the Resistance movement during the occupation of Athens by the Germans during the Second World War. Tinged with tragedy, this is a moving portrayal of the starvation and deprivation war brings.

IR 9+

TITLE INDEX

The number refers to the entry not the page.

SUBJECT INDEX

Books have been indexed under the specific subject(s) they cover. If they are set in a particular period but without a specific subject, then they have been indexed under the country in chronological order (for example England, Elizabeth I (1558–1603)). There are references to the more specific topics. The name England has been used for all of English/British history as it was felt to be more useful to keep all of the historical periods in one sequence rather than split them between the two names. Books have also been indexed under place if it was thought this would be useful.

The number refers to the entry not the page.